HIGHWAY

50

HIGHWAY
50
Ain't That America

JIM LILLIEFORS

FULCRUM PUBLISHING
Golden, Colorado

Library of Congress Cataloging-in-Publication Data

Lilliefors, Jim.
    Highway 50 : ain't that America / Jim Lilliefors.
      p.   cm.
    ISBN 1-55591-073-4
    1. United States—Description and travel—1981– 2. United States
Highway 50. 3. United States—Social life and customs—1971–
4. Lilliefors, Jim, 1955-   —Journeys—United States.   I. Title.
E169.04.L55   1993
917.304'928—dc20   92-54766
                                                               CIP

Printed in the United States of America
0 9 8 7 6 5 4 3 2

Fulcrum Publishing
350 Indiana Street, Suite 350
Golden, CO 80401–5093

For Linda and Glory

Contents

Acknowledgments

Thanks to the many people along the way who spent time telling their tales.

A special thank you to Pat Frederick, who took interest in this project several years ago, offered valuable encouragement and wielded a heavy red pencil.

And thanks to many others:

Pam Leppin, whose enthusiasm inspired the idea.

Co-pilots, who traveled with me, including Patty Sheppard, Linda and Ryan Magana, Laura Kauper.

My father, the secretary of transportation.

My brother, commerce secretary and brutal critic.

Dave Paulin, for those long conversations on the boardwalk, during which he told me exactly how this book should be written.

Numerous people who offered advice and who helped with research, including Lisa Daniels and Beth Mariner.

The invaluable assistance of Richard Weingroff.

Carmel Huestis and all the good people at Fulcrum.

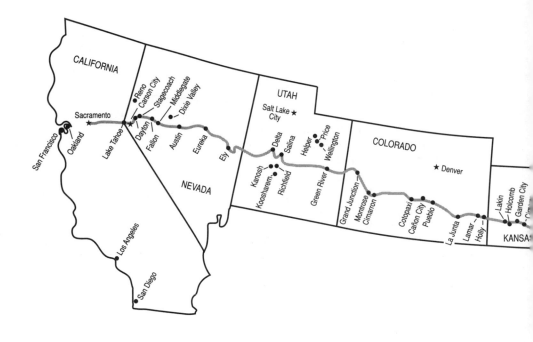

Highway 50
Ocean City, Maryland, to Sacramento, California

The great gifts are not got by analysis.
Everything good is on the highway.
—Ralph Waldo Emerson

HIGHWAY
50

The Sign

I t came to me on a warm spring morning while driving in sea mist alongside the Atlantic that far too much had been taken for granted. The sign. Every day for nearly a decade, I had passed beneath a highway sign at the southern end of Ocean City, Maryland, the town where I live, that reads: "Sacramento 3073." Five thousand passes, and the sign was part of the scenery. Like the barnacle-encrusted anchors at the edge of the inlet, which I also did not really see anymore, or the fishing shanties that lined the harbor.

On that mild morning in March, however, I took notice again. The sign's message burned through the mist and fog as if I had never seen it before, and the sea breeze, drifting faintly from the northeast, seemed to carry a scent of other seasons. I felt a pull toward different landscapes, toward more lucid dreams.

It was time. Instead of driving to work, I stopped at my bank on the mainland and closed out my account. I placed the money in the bottom of a rusty tackle box in the trunk of the old Ford. And then I began driving west, into the brightening haze of a Monday morning. Past the familiar exit to the familiar life. After fifteen years in journalism, I had been contemplating this move for weeks. Trading in my stable but increasingly monotonous role as a small-town newspaper editor for a life on the road. Going, slowly, where Highway 50 goes.

For years my home had been on the eastern end of 50, the centralmost of the transcontinental U.S. routes and probably the least appreciated. Only highway historians and a few old-timers seem to know the significance of Highway 50, a route that traces most of the major pioneer trails as it makes its way west; a road that changes its name to Main Street in a majority of the towns it passes through.

"As much as any highway, Route 50 tells the history of how this country developed," Richard Weingroff, a writer with the Federal Highway Administration, once told me. But ask anyone about great U.S. highways, and they'll mention Route 66. Or Highway 40. Or U.S. 1.

Highway 50's golden years were in the 1950s, when you could stop at any motor court along the way and find brochures that touted the road's importance:

"Fast and thoroughly modern, avoiding the extremes of heat and cold."

"No one has fully enjoyed America who has not traveled Famous Fifty. America's Central Pleasure Route."

"See it all on Highway 50, America's All-Year Playground."

The brochures cluttered the front seat of the old Ford as I left town. This was the Highway 50 I would travel—a link of historic trails that had spawned towns and commerce routes, that helped nurture the nation. But also a pleasure route that hasn't changed significantly in years—and where a quiet rebellion is taking place.

Along this transcontinental Main Street, which before the interstates came along was a major thoroughfare across the country, the stories one hears—the things people tell each other and themselves—are different. Traditions survive. I decided as I drove west that I would listen, in remote prairie settlements and mountain hamlets, through rich, rolling farmland and dying mining towns. Where stories we have forgotten, or never heard, are still told.

It's 7:40 A.M. Twenty miles out. An Exxon sign glows. I pull to a stop beside the pumps. The bluish, flickering lights hum, fields of corn stubble glisten and a filmy rain clings to a distant stand of pines. The lights look garish beside the cornfield. As the old Ford feeds, the attendant watches from a doorway, pretending to count money under the fluorescent glare. He's sensing, I imagine, that I am not where I ought to be at this time of the morning.

Everything is accentuated so early in the day—the sound of truck tires on the highway, the smell of gasoline. I walk to a pay phone and call the office to say I won't be coming in. The distracted matter-of-factness of the receptionist's reply is startling: "Okay, well, thanks for calling in. I hope you feel better." (I had not said anything about feeling bad.)

The attendant watches as I return.

"What's it supposed to be like?" I ask, handing him a ten.

"Excuse me?"

"The weather."

"Cooler tonight," he says, looking me up and down. "Then real cold tomorrow."

"How cold?"

"Thirties."

This is bad news, if true. But I decide not to worry about it. Such are the thoughts that prevent detours from being taken. He's still counting money as I pull the old Ford into gear and head west. I wave to him.

Were she capable of thought, the old Ford would probably have approved of this escape, with the caveat that we take it slowly. A complicated and quirky machine, an old blue LTD, she had traveled reliably up and down these sandy beach roads for years. I kept her because there was no good reason not to. People give up on cars— like everything else—too quickly these days.

Which isn't to say that age doesn't at times make her difficult. Very occasionally, for no real reason, she will refuse to start. If I

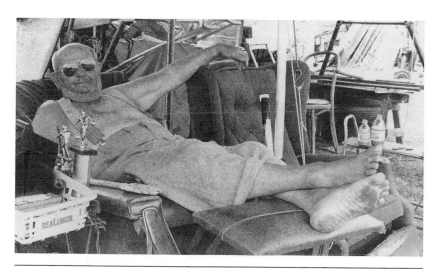

Straughn Smack, relaxing outside his home along Route 50 near Willards, Maryland: "You see an awful lot of things just sitting out here."

take her to the three mechanics in town, I will receive three different explanations (each told with great authority, each requiring substantial garage work). So I let her rest, and she usually revives herself. Her troubles can be traced to her dubious origins. She had been custom-made years ago at a local garage, mostly from old parts. Nearly everyone who ever looked beneath the hood remarked that something was wrong, that the engine did not seem to be put together right. I call it her birth defect. It, too, is now taken for granted.

For miles the road is flanked by farmland. There are cows and horses in the wet rolling fields where sun gleams low in the pines. The mist is rich with a smell of earth and fertilizer. Near the town of Willards is the house where Marvel and Straughn Smack live. Straughn, sitting out front already, waves as I go by. I wave back.

The Smack brothers are in their mid-sixties and have never been off of Maryland's Eastern Shore. Since his stroke, Straughn spends most of his time on a rusted metal chair beside Highway 50, waving at the traffic. His brother Marvel still cleans chicken coops for a living. When he isn't working, he sits inside and listens to the radio. The Smacks rent their house for $12 a month.

Farther up the road is John Calloway's farm and produce stand. This early in the spring the stand is boarded up while the Calloways work seed drills in the fields behind it, planting their crops. In another few weeks John's mother, Bly, will open the produce stand to sell preserves, embroideries and knickknacks. Bly is eighty-one. She lives in a farmhouse on the other side of Highway 50 with a cat and a peacock. Every July, when the peacock sheds, she sells its plumes for two dollars apiece.

Living beside the highway, the Calloways have seen the world change. "Highway's what brought all the people here," Bly Calloway told me one morning as we shared a fresh melon. "Used to be nobody knew we were here, and that wasn't such a bad thing."

It is not long—less than three hours—before the old Ford's first mute protest occurs. Near Cambridge, where the Choptank River joins the Chesapeake Bay, her engine light comes on. I know from past experience what this means—nearly anything— and decide to take a detour onto the old Eastern Shore. We go easy, down two-lane roads covered with sand and oyster shells, in search of a stopping place.

Bly Calloway and a crop of Eastern Shore melons. "People started coming in," she says, "with the highway. Can't do nothing about that. It connected this area with the rest of the world, I guess you could say." Photo by Ron Angle.

The mist is gone. Along the back bays and marshes and cattail swamps, the air has a tang of salt and seafood. This is a land that beats slowly to the pulse of nature; it is also a factory, producing corn, soybeans, crabs and oysters in enormous numbers. Each year 225 million blue crabs are taken from Chesapeake Bay waters, more than anywhere in the world. Those from Maryland sell for forty million dollars. Oysters bring in eleven million dollars. Twenty thousand farms on the Shore account for 80 percent of the state's corn, soybean and wheat crops.

We come eventually to the tiny town of Tilghman Island,

where I stop for a late lunch at the Harrison Inn. The year is turning, starting over again. All along the shore now, water is reoxygenating, luring blue crabs out of the channels toward the oxygen-rich eel grass of the shoal areas. In backwater inlets nearby, herons and egrets are building their nests.

A man at the bar walks over to the window next to where I'm seated sipping a beer and asks what I think. The old life, the one I had lived for fifteen years, seems to have burned off as quickly as the mist.

"About what?"

He nods out the window at the marina. "She's gonna turn tonight, looks like. Say she's got a nor'easter coming in."

I move my chair to face the water, to see exactly what it is he's talking about.

"Gonna be cold again for a few."

"How many?"

"Hard to tell. Could pass by and be fine at the end of the week. Hard to predict what she's gonna do."

He grunts and goes back to the bar.

After lunch I walk down the road to the Fairbanks Tackle Shop in the bright, late-afternoon light. There's a smell of fish and oysters in the breeze. Out in the marina the docked boats make a regular sound on the pilings, their ropes creaking against the old wood. I sit there on a bench in the shade for a long, long time, watching sunlight change patterns on the water.

The stillness is broken at one point by a woman walking down the road from the seafood house, her sandals making a quick clicking sound on the pavement. Oil stains glow in the sun.

"Say there's cold air coming in," she says cheerfully, by way of greeting.

"That's what I hear."

"Don't know why it can't stay like this."

Later, in the tackle shop, after the wind has turned cool, the men are all talking about the weather. One says he's "afraid she gonna turn by morning."

Several men are playing pool, and those who aren't are sitting on benches, talking. The day turns to dusk.

"Say she's blowin' up to New England," one of the sitting men says.

"She be here. That's what Wadey said."

I ask these men, most of whom earn their living on the water, how the oyster business is. But they do not have much to say about it.

"Best thing you could do," one of them says, "is get out there and see it for yourself. Get in an honest day's work."

It provokes friendly laughter.

I'm still in Fairbanks Tackle when Wade Murphy comes in wearing a soiled, green jumpsuit and the solemn expression of all longtime watermen. Someone tells him that I'm asking questions. Murphy sizes me up grimly.

"Well, if you're so curious, get up here at five then, and come on out."

"Five in the morning?"

"Five sharp."

There is subdued levity at Fairbanks Tackle.

I tell him okay, figuring the first rule of being a passive adventurer is to accept invitations. It's the only way to really hear what an oysterman has to say.

The old Ford's familiar shape stays on the edge of the inn's gravel parking lot that night. It is reassuring.

Before going to sleep, I take a walk in the cool stillness of the pines, hearing water, thinking about the other life, the one I had traded in that morning. Most of the old Victorian-style houses are dark, although in some of the windows television sets flicker behind curtains.

An Honest Day

The sky is full of stars when lights go on at Fairbanks Tackle Shop. The weather has indeed turned. An icy wind gusts over the inlet and rattles the sailboat masts.

"She's blowing," one of the men inside says as I pull the door closed. His breath becomes a shimmer in the air. Coffee steams from a styrofoam cup.

"You sure you want to go out?" another asks. Grinning at what I don't know.

"Got two more days, Wadey," another fellow says.

"That'll get it."

"Get twenty bushels, she may come in okay."

"She'll die down, Wadey."

I stand there shivering and listening, watching the bobbing boat masts. After several minutes, Wade Murphy makes a grunting noise and leaves the store. "Better you get on out there," I'm told, matter-of-factly. "He ain't going to wait on you." The others chuckle. Five minutes later I am on the deck of the *Rebecca T. Ruark* as it churns in the dark toward open water at a steady eight knots.

Below, a three-man crew is sleeping on short wooden benches, their faces lit by the blue flames of a propane stove. I stand beside Murphy as he steers. The air is so cold it stings my lungs. "Do you have spare gloves?" There is a lengthy silence before this little man in the green jumpsuit lets me borrow a pair. He admonishes me for not bringing any. "You should have thought of that before you come out," he says, and turns away. The gloves are crusty, and they smell of fish.

The *Rebecca Ruark* is the oldest skipjack on the Chesapeake Bay, part of the nation's oldest sailing fleet. Skipjacks—majestic, wooden, fifty-foot sloops—were designed around 1890 as a more efficient oyster dredge boat than the two-masted rig bugeyes then commonly in use. What keeps Chesapeake skipjacks going these days, I soon realize, is the stubbornness of people like Murphy, who has been oystering from Tilghman Island for thirty-two winters and intends to do so for twenty-five more.

When I tell Wade Murphy I've heard stories about the demise of the skipjack, he seems genuinely offended. "Shit, where'd you hear that? That's what you get from reading newspapers. That's what the scientists say. Hell, scientists said we're going to be extinct in a year or two. They don't know. Watermen know things scientists can't imagine." He stares straight ahead as the boat cuts across open water, and I decide to say no more on this subject. "You'd have to be pretty fucking dumb to listen to a scientist before you'd listen to an oysterman," he says. Behind us, in the trailing yawlboat, a diesel engine rattles low and steady.

By the time we near Plum Point, on the Western Shore, the crew is on deck, and the water is suddenly bright with a sheen of sun. Bay dipper ducks dive below the surface looking for food.

"Least it's a nice day," one of the crew members says. It still seems unbearably cold to me. "You should've come out with us in the middle of winter, when the bay was all froze up."

The crew members are from Crisfield, and this is their first winter dredging. They're young—seventeen, twenty-four and twenty-six—and defer easily to the captain. Murphy, they each tell me in brief, furtive, one-on-one conversations, can read the bay as well as anyone alive. He knows where the oyster beds are, where the shallow water ends and the channels begin. "When you've been at it as long as Wade has, you can read the water like a book," one of the crew members says.

The captain catches his eye as he says this and scowls. All is quiet again. Picking a spot, Murphy slows the boat to three knots, and crew members throw out the two forty-four-inch metal dredges, one on either side. For three minutes—or until Murphy can tell from the tug on the boat that they're full—the dredges drag bottom. They're pulled up then by hydraulic winch and dumped on deck. The crew has three minutes to cull, separating the "keepers" from the "trash"—rocks, shells, soda-pop bottles, blue crabs and "boxes," shells with dead oysters inside. This is the pattern that continues until sundown, almost without break, the oyster shells collecting in four piles on the boat's pinewood deck. I help them cull for a while but only get in the way.

"Why don't you just watch," Murphy finally suggests.

I nod and take a seat on the side rail of the boat, my vantage point for the next several hours.

All day long the cold March winds whitecap the water. The crew members seem oblivious to the cold, the awful tedium of oystering.

As they work, Murphy talks, still angry it seems over my remark about the death of old-style oystering. "Give Mother Nature a chance," he says, "and we'll be okay. All these fucking scientists say it's so bad. I've seen a lot of young oysters out there this winter. I think they're coming back. In two years, I think it'll be a lot better.

"You learn where they grow and where they don't. But only from being out here. If you're talking about aquaculture, that's the worst fucking thing they could do. This is a profession for people who understand the water. The scientists don't understand a fucking thing about the water. They don't know the cycles. Only way you can understand it is being out all your life doing it."

Despite Murphy's know-how, he has a tough time today finding a good spot. By the Western Shore, he is turning the boat in wide circles, but the catches are only about thirty or forty oysters per dredge. At a good spot, he'd be getting a hundred.

"Ain't finding much yet," he says to me gruffly.

"Why?"

He waits before speaking, as if it's not an answer he's giving but another comment.

"Everything's been worked so much. We're getting too many shells in here." He adds, "It's distracting having someone on board who's not helping."

"Are you going to try another spot?"

"We're in the edge of the mud," he says, ignoring the question. "So I got a dredge down for that. Not as light as a mud dredge but lighter'n a round bar."

"It's not doing the trick, I guess."

"The thing people don't understand," he goes on, "is that the water is always good if you're willing to work. The newspapers have decided oystering is dying because it makes a good story. But what people don't understand is supply and demand. The oyster catch may be way down, but the price is way up. So it don't make no difference. A hundred years ago, fifteen million bushels come out of the Chesapeake. Ten years ago it was two million. Last year it was less than half a million. But back in the early seventies, when I was bringing in all those oysters, they was going for three or four bucks a bushel. This winter, they been as high as thirty-two bucks."

By late morning Murphy has found a good spot, and soon Aaron Lankford is counting one hundred oysters out of the left-side dredge. The bay ducks are diving quicker now, eating the food that we're dredging up. The sun is high, but the winds stay snappy.

Murphy seems pleased. After ignoring me for a good hour, he turns and offers a proud smile.

"It just takes a little while longer some days to find the spot," he says.

Within twenty minutes, though, the wind picks up. A bad sign for the afternoon. Murphy stops talking to me again. He gets on the radio.

Wade Murphy, captain of the Rebecca T. Ruark, *a skipjack on the* Chesapeake Bay.

"Wadey, she's kicking now," another boat captain says.

"How far, Dickey?"

"She's up to twelve."

"We're only to four."

"She may be there, Wadey."

"We been holding her at four, Dickey. Where are you?"

Soon, the bay begins to breeze up, and the radio conversation resumes:

"How much you got now, Wadey?"

"Five now, Dickey. But she's cutting against it."

"I was afraid that was coming."

In a few minutes: "We're getting ten, Dickey."

"Got it bad enough without the wind."

"I know it, Dickey."

The wind is now strong enough that the dredges won't stay on the bottom anymore, and the boat rocks in the swells. I lose my balance at one point, standing by the wheel, and fall against Murphy. He immediately grabs my arms, and throws me across the boat. "Fucking newspaperman, next thing you know, you're going to hit the throttle."

For several minutes I stand off to the side, looking away. The crew members seem embarrassed. Politeness, while fine on land, has no place out here. Murphy tells me to go below deck. It is a bitter lesson. Sitting shivering beside the propane stove, I contemplate my own fields of expertise and realize how worthless they are in this world of the water.

While I'm down there, out of the wind, the three crew members come down separately to make their lunches. Each does the same: gets two slices of Wonder Bread from a cooler, takes out a piece of ham and smothers it with salt and pepper. That and a Pepsi is the meal. All three are cordial, though they treat me as something of an interloper.

"What makes things bad is the tide's cutting against it," Aaron Lankford says, as he fixes his sandwich.

"How long?"

"I can't read it, but she'll be for a while. What brought you out?"

"Wanted to see what it was like."

"Well, now you know."

I ask about the oyster business, and he grins. "Nah, it's all right. This goes back with us six, seven generations. My grandfather'll tell you it's always been rough. Ain't no different now."

"Water ages you," Kenny Welch says when he comes for his ham on Wonder Bread. "Can add twenty years to some people."

"But they stay at it."

"Oh, it'd only age you on the outside," he says, and laughs. "You see some people's only thirty and they look like an old man. But they'll keep doing it."

"It's tough," says Jerry Lankford, Aaron's older brother, pouring pepper onto his ham. "Because whatever you make on the water, you got to put back into it. And every good season is followed by a bad one."

"So you never get ahead?"

"Not by much. But that's the way it is. You're not coming out again tomorrow, are you?"

"I'm not sure," I say.

The wind is up to twenty knots now. Murphy steers the boat back across the bay, giving up on the Western Shore. For the first time he has the sail raised to stabilize the sixty-foot mast.

I come out from below deck, feeling a little sick from the fumes of the propane stove. As the boat cuts through the rough waves, I see that no one is at the wheel. I search for Murphy and find that he's at the rail, urinating overboard.

"Tide's moving against the wind," he explains, seeing me and turning slightly as his pee arcs into the bay. "You better stay below deck."

I decide to stay where I am. "We heading back to the Eastern Shore?"

"Cooper's Holler," he says sternly, zipping up.

"Are we through oystering?"

No answer. The deck dries off in the sun as we cross over turbulent waters. The two of us stand by the wheel. There's a strong briny smell of oyster shells in the breeze. "Look out," he says at one point, deliberately trying to put me in the way.

When we reach Cooper's Holler, the sun is dropping and the winds are frigid again. Murphy cuts the engines, the dredges go out. Off in the distance are the outlines of the Bay Bridge—

Highway 50, leading off of the Shore. The catches are soon up to a hundred again, which means Murphy will keep us out until sundown. The light turns orange over pink-blue waters, in the window of the galley and the faces of the crew. The spray is icy cold. When the sun finally disappears, Murphy tells the crew to stop, and he makes a prediction: "Thirty-five, thirty-eight."

By the time we reach Tilghman, the stars are out again, and I feel queasy from the pitch of the waves. Murphy docks at Harrison Oyster Company, where I am heartened by the familiar shape of the old Ford, alone at the edge of the parking lot.

The day's catch is shoveled into metal buckets that swing on pulleys onto the dock. I watch as a man in a glass booth counts them. "Thirty-eight bushels," he announces. Murphy nods. Thirty-eight. A subdued triumph. I return the crusty gloves and thank him, but there is no response. This is not the life I will trade mine for.

As I walk away, I can't help thinking that in only nine hours Murphy and his crew will leave the channel again, moving at a steady eight knots toward open waters.

Tastee 29

The Chesapeake is specked with sails as the old Ford cruises quietly to Maryland's Western Shore in the bright, cool morning. A day's rest has served its purpose: The engine light stays off through the sprawling, jumbled suburbs of Annapolis and Washington.

In the capital, 50 becomes Constitution Avenue, passing the Washington Monument, the Vietnam Veterans Memorial, the Lincoln Memorial. The highway shares names and numbers as it leaves Washington for Virginia: U.S. 50, Route 29, Lee Highway. Anxious to get away from the traffic and souvenir sellers, I drive on to Fairfax, where old and new mesh like gigantic objects of modern art—mirror-sided office buildings reflect the sky, block sunlight from the dingy strip stores and old motels with names like Hiway 50 Motel, All States Motel, Hy-Way Motel ("Color TV by RCA"). Pieces of different eras sharing space.

At the Tastee 29, the stools are chrome-rimmed, and the tabletops are a marblelike formica. At each booth is a Tri-Vue wall jukebox. A song by the Judds called "She Deserves Him" is playing. The waitress smiles, chomping gum, handing me a menu. "You got a sunburn, didn't you? How'd you get that this time of year?"

"Oystering," I say.

"Uh-huh."

I ask if I can still order breakfast. "You can do whatever you want," she says. "Only things you can't do here is snap your fingers at me or whistle. 'Cause I don't answer to that tune."

"Fair enough."

Outside, the traffic goes by quickly. The promise that was in the spring air two days earlier is nowhere in these gusts that rattle the window. I order a mushroom omelet with home fries.

Jannet—"That's with two 'n's," she says—sits across from me. "God," she says, and exhales for about twenty seconds.

She's dressed in Levis and a blue, lace-frill top with a Harley Davidson insignia. I seem to be the only one here she doesn't know. "You don't mind if I sit just a few minutes to rest my feet, do you?" She pulls out a pack of Marlboros. I tell her no, I don't.

"So, oystering, huh? Catch any?"

"Thirty-eight bushels."

She puts her gum in the ashtray and lights up a cigarette, not sure how to respond. "You wouldn't believe the half of this," she says, nodding toward the men at the counter. "Some very good people, though," she adds.

"Are they?"

"Oh, yeah. I've been here more than ten years. Made some good friends." She nods slightly, so I nod. "I mean, most of the people—not all, but most—are on a first-name basis. And some even have nicknames for theirselves.

"I had a couple from Kentucky the other week who tipped me seven dollars on an eight-dollar tab," she goes on. "They told me they'd never had a waitress smile like that before. That makes you feel good." At the recollection she pulls back and smiles, then turns to check the clock. "Just waiting for Pops now," she says. I do not ask who Pops is, hoping she will notice that another order has come up. No such luck.

Apparently, sitting with the customers is a part of her job. As she smokes, I look around the diner, and two things catch my eye: what seems to be a bullet hole in the window a few inches from my face, and a series of letters above the door to the kitchen: "YCJCYAQFTJB." The men at the counter eye me several times as the air sizzles with the sound of hamburger and sausage browning on the grill.

Pops, she explains, is an older man, a widower, who shows up in the afternoons to help out, busing tables and washing dishes. "We take care of him," she says. "You know. We feed him. He's just a nice man. A lot of people don't have nothing else 'cept this place."

Finally Jannet notices that my food is ready and brings it over. The portions are huge, the fries browned and crispy, the toast generously buttered. It's all served on a blue plate. I eat slowly, thankful that she has at last left me in peace.

The Tastee 29 diner in Fairfax, Virginia: "A lot of people don't have nothing else 'cept this place," says waitress Jannet Emery.

Diners. Forty years ago, the country had ten thousand. Now there are about two thousand, although that number has held steady for ten years.

When I finish, I leave a three-dollar tip and pay at the register.

"So, you from around here?" Jannet asks, taking a good look at me for the first time.

"Nope. We're from east of here. We just decided to leave everything behind and take to the road. Now we're going west of here. Old Isabel's never seen the West before."

Sometimes, for conversational purposes, I call the old Ford Isabel.

"Oh, I'm sure she'll like it," Jannet says, looking out at the parking lot.

"I think so."

I can resist no more and ask what those letters above the door to the kitchen mean.

"You sure you want me to tell you?" she says, popping gum super fast and grinning.

"Go ahead."

"It means 'Your Curiosity Just Cost You A Quarter For The Juke Box.'"

"Oh."

The crooked-toothed smile, the lightning-fast chew. I give it to her and she calls back to one of the men by the jukebox. "Hey, put on two forty-two."

Then to me, surprisingly soft-spoken, she explains, "That's Conway."

Clean and Honest People

Outside of Fairfax, U.S. 50 narrows to two lanes and becomes John S. Mosby Highway, named for the Confederate ranger whose guerrilla army once sabotaged Union operations in this rolling countryside. Every few miles now, old metal signs recount what happened here during the Civil War. I pull the Ford to a stop beside each one we come to and rest. The journey will be leisurely. I will not miss things.

"Near this spot, Jackson's men sank down to rest on July 17, 1861, without placing pickets. Said Jackson, 'Let the poor fellows sleep. I will guard the camp myself.'"

"Here Lee turned north," reads another, "and moved toward Dranesville and Leesburg on the Ox Road. The Army entered Maryland Sept. 5–6, 1862." Near a place called Chantilly, the land rises and crests, and, suddenly, only for a moment, miles of countryside come into view among the trees: a verdant valley, plowed-over cornfields and hazy, timbered slopes. The sudden transition in landscape stops me. I make a U-turn and go back, parking on the gravel road–shoulder and staring out at the still, sprawling earth. I sit on the hood of the old Ford, becoming intoxicated by the breeze that has turned warm again, a kind of metaphor. Seldom is so much visible from one spot, it seems.

After several minutes, though, I realize that I am not alone. A short, grizzly man has parked his tractor in the field and is walking toward me with determined steps. He seems to be gripping something.

"Howdy," he says, looking with disapproval at the Ford. Cars whisk by on Highway 50.

"Can't park here?" I ask.

He shakes his head, meaning it's okay.

The sky shifts. Clouds drift by in the breeze. He opens his fist and displays a small piece of metal.

"Musket ball," he says. He hands it over, grinning.

"Musket ball? From the Civil War?"

"Yep. That's right. Still find a few of them."

He takes it back.

The man's name is Calvin Alexander, and he tells me proudly that he's found several dozen musket balls during the forty years he's lived in his house near Chantilly. We both stare for a while longer at the piece of metal in his hand while, in the windy shade, phone wires whistle faintly.

Up the road, trees darken in the dusk. By a stoplight near Lee's Corner, a long-haired, shirtless man with a Grateful Dead tattoo on his chest is hitchhiking. There is no traffic except for the old Ford, and when I stop for the light he comes over and opens the passenger door.

"I wasn't stopping," I say.

"What?"

"I wasn't stopping."

There's a surprised look in his eyes. He's hugging a wet paper bag that smells of beer. "What?"

"I said I wasn't stopping. I was stopping for the light."

He hugs the bag tighter. "I'm only going down the road."

He starts to get in, and I look around to see if there are any other cars coming. In all directions it's quiet and empty. I can hear the traffic light click as it turns red again.

"How far?"

"Just about six miles, man," he says.

The light becomes green and the man sits down, waiting for me to nod so he can close the door.

"Okay."

"Solid."

Ahead, the road winds over a hill into Aldie, an old, wooded mill stop with stone bridges and open-front antique shops. There's a sound of creek water and birds in the Virginia countryside.

"You want a beer, man?" the hitchhiker asks.

"No, thanks."

The smell of him is strong. Beer and sweat and soiled bluejeans. There is a knife, I see, in a sheath attached to his belt. He hums as we go, tapping his fingers on his legs and on the seat, and tosses back his hair, then lets it fall forward again in rhythm to his humming. I look over at him several times, struck by how he seems to resemble Jay Leno. A long-haired version.

"Where are you headed to, man?" he asks as we approach Middleburg.

"No destination," I say.

"Solid."

He drinks a beer as we pass through Middleburg and opens another in the horse country west of it.

"Just driving?"

"Just driving."

"That's solid."

"Where are you headed? You said six miles," I say, noticing that we've gone eleven.

He laughs as though I had told a joke.

"Man, don't get on me about distances. That's, like, not exactly my thing, man."

I wait for him to say more, but he doesn't. He slides a hand over his stomach, still grinning, looking out the side window. After another mile the humming resumes.

Huge estates appear in the countryside, clusters of trees, cows, horses. Occasionally a gas station or market, always with a rusted, round Coca-Cola sign. Near Winchester we come to a roadside lounge called the Silver Dollar, and the hitchhiker gathers his moist beer bag and pulls it to his chest.

"Check it out, man," he says.

"Pardon?"

I'm not sure at first if he wants me to stop or just to look. There are six or seven motorcycles parked outside.

"This is where you're going?"

"This is cool, man," he says.

Before leaving, he shakes my hand and asks, "You sure you don't want a beer?"

Again I decline. But as I drive off into a fresh, darkening hill country, I find myself wondering why I felt so apprehensive about having a hitchhiker in the car.

The air becomes cooler ahead, and the old Ford begins to make strange sounds, clattering, it seems, in time to the country music on WINC radio. A motel in town advertises "Special Rates

For Clean and Honest People." The Tourist City Motel. An old brick building with a neon sign that blinks erratically across the highway. There are three other cars in the parking lot: West Virginia, Vermont, South Carolina.

The clerk looks me over, then bows slightly. He announces that I will be eligible for the special rate. He's a middle-aged Asian man, who smells slightly of body odor.

"How do you know that I'm honest?"

"How do I know?" He waves away the question as if it were a joke and gives me the key. "Sometimes it's better not to ask questions," he says.

In the motel room I pour a drink, turn on the television and ponder this wisdom. Humphrey Bogart is chastising Peter Lorre, but it is difficult to pay attention because of the people next door. They are playing country music tapes loudly and laughing.

I wake several times in the night and hear the music thumping as I reach for my watch.

3:14 A.M.: "There's something fishy going on on all those fishing trips you been going on."

4:43 A.M.: "You say we tried and it's over, but honey, it's only over for you."

5:01 A.M.: "I'm sitting here sipping on my second beer, just working on making your heavenly body all mine."

Still later it is light outside, and I sit up startled, hearing a woman's urgent shouts. A bed is squeaking rhythmically, banging against the wall. "Don't stop, don't stop!" she yells.

Afterward, there is dead silence.

I lie there and listen to the breeze flapping the screen, the sound of trucks going by. Virginia air. When I fall asleep again, the sleep is all dreams, strange dreams about hitchhikers and motorcycles and Jay Leno doing his show out of a motel room in the Virginia hillside. In the real morning it is sunny and nice, and the bloom of spring is in the wind. The real music.

The old Ford's clatter worsens. The engine shakes and then the whole body. The country music sounds as though it has been reinterpreted by an oompah band. Back out along Highway 50, she won't go faster than thirty, and the drivers of other cars shake their heads as they pass me.

At last I stop and summon a Winchester mechanic.

He's a short, skeptical man with a boyish face, a gigantic belly and thick, hairy arms that are too short. For several minutes he stares down into the engine, chewing gum.

"She heating up on you?"

"She's rattling."

"She heating up?"

"Not really."

He leans over into the engine and taps on a spring coil just below the carburetor. He stands up shaking his head but still looking.

"What is it?" I say.

He checks some more, touches a few parts, chews gum, wipes his hands, touches a few more parts, wipes his hands and then finally looks me square in the eyes: "How long you been driving without your exhaust valve?"

I swallow.

"Exhaust valve?"

He indicates the hole beneath the carburetor, where, indeed, an exhaust valve is missing.

"Dangerous business," he says.

"Can you fix it?"

He chews gum for a long time, staring down at the engine.

"Possibly get to it tomorrow," he says. "Monday at the latest."

"How dangerous is it driving like that?"

Again he chews and stares, for close to a minute, as if trying to properly phrase his reply.

"Well. I wouldn't drive her around the block with that kind of fire hazard inherent," he says, wiping his hands again. "This is raw exhaust here, right below your carburetor. All she has to do is get a spark and you got a fire."

"But how likely is it to get a spark?"

Chew, stare. Chew, stare.

"Well, it's possible you could go another twenty miles like that. But I'm not going to tell you to do it because you might get to the corner right here and have the goddamn engine blow up. And I don't want that kind of thing on my hands."

Now we both stare at the engine. The prospect of the old Ford dying such a spectacular death—an explosion in Winchester,

Virginia—is unnerving. But there is something disagreeable about this mechanic, and I decide to find a gas station.

The mechanic there is an amiable, wiry old man named Gus. He puts his hand down into the engine where the exhaust valve should be and asks, "What happened?"

"I guess it fell off."

"Well, we'll just have to order another one, then."

"How long will it take?"

"Oh, could be a day or two before it gets here."

"Okay."

Before leaving, I ask him about the fire hazard, and he grins. "No, sir, there's practically no danger of a fire. Just cause you a lot of noise, that's all."

The next several days I spend in Winchester, taking long walks down country roads, enjoying the spring breezes. Each morning I buy a newspaper at the Winchester Valley News and Novelties in the old brick section of town. In his store, Jim Devine has more than five hundred baseball caps hanging on wires from the ceiling. He says he began collecting them "just as something to do." Now people bring him caps from all over the country. His little store has become, he says, legendary. "It's taken on a life of its own, I guess."

When I come in each day, he asks the same thing: "Enjoying Winchester?"

I tell him I am.

"Where you going to walk today?"

"Not sure. Any suggestions?"

Without the car I feel suddenly anchored to this old town, once a strategic Civil War stronghold. There is no easy exit anymore. The smell of boxwood and spring flowers, the layout of the streets—Winchester becomes familiar, a place I know. Most of my walks take me through downtown, past the old building on Braddock Street where George Washington worked as a surveyor, and up the hill to Mount Hebron Cemetery, where I sit in the cool shade of Douglas fir and cedar and read the newspaper among the limestone tombs of old Virginia families.

Comment on the culture: Tombstones today list only two pieces of information, beginning and end. A hundred years ago they told stories. Beneath the limestone slab that juts crookedly from the grass across from me one morning is buried a boy, Willie Lockart. On the faded stone: "Our pride and joy of life forever fled, When we know our darling son is dead." It is signed J and Amanda Lockart. Next to him is buried Amanda, who thirty-seven years later "gained the rest at last, For which was often sighed, Fears no more life's chilly blast, Though broken heart she died."

Nearby, rows of three-foot-tall gray stones mark the graves of Confederate soldiers. A separate, Confederate cemetery. Virginia split into two states over the Civil War, and many people down here still display Confederate flags on their pickups, as if trying to preserve some ideal of the South. As if the Civil War had not been largely about slavery.

I stop at the Rebel Lounge one night and meet a woman named Patty, who is herself somewhat of a wanderer. An open, disarmingly serious woman, she sits at the bar flanked by a group of Virginia hillbillies and tells me about herself as she chainsmokes Marlboro Lights. Patty grew up in North Carolina, she says, became pregnant at age seventeen.

"I guess I spent the last fifteen years running from guilt. I came from a Catholic family, and I guess it was some kind of rebellion. I don't understand it even now."

She's a tall, awkward woman with short black hair and large green eyes, who is dressed like an inner-city teenager: sleeveless T-shirt, black jeans and sneakers. Several times as she talks she knocks coasters onto the floor with her elbow; once a napkin sticks to her arm for several minutes before I point it out and she pulls it away.

On television there's an episode of "Murder, She Wrote," and most of the men sitting at the bar stare, although there is no sound.

"So do you live in Winchester now?" I ask, trying to speed up the chronology of her past, to bring her to the present.

"I'm visiting my brother," she says. "My son lives with him. My brother and his wife. Everyone's happy with the arrangement. I don't see anything wrong with it, really. People have preconceived notions about what you're supposed to do and what you're not supposed to do. Like, I don't see anything wrong with a woman going by herself to a bar." She waves her cigarette in the air to indicate that this, in fact, is what she has done. "It doesn't mean she's looking to get laid. I mean, in some people's eyes it might. But that's their problem."

The more she drinks, the more her southern accent comes out and the more friendly she becomes. Like a lot of other strangers, she seems to like my not talking much.

"I'm thinking of going back to school, I guess. I worked as a waitress for years, but I wasn't very good at it. I wasn't very good at marriage, either. Or relationships. But I think someday I can do something. So where are you going?"

"No destination."

"Have you been to Middleburg?"

"I drove through."

"That's a good destination." She smokes very seriously for a while, then adds, examining the cigarette as she pulls it to her mouth, "I'll show it to you tomorrow if you like."

There is dancing later, after "Murder, She Wrote" ends. Patty and I watch. One young couple sways slightly, hugging each other tight, and occasionally petting. An older man does the Twist with a woman half his age. Two old ladies are dancing together, one of them self-consciously, as if she is walking in place.

Patty drives me back to the Tourist City Motel and agrees to pick me up the next morning at nine o'clock. As I stand outside in the lot, country music playing again from the room next door, the telephone wires are humming. Winchester is suddenly pulsing with energy, with new life.

The Main Street

A noisy brown Toyota is idling in the parking lot at twenty minutes after nine the next morning. Through a crack in the curtains I see Patty, wearing sunglasses and smoking, nodding her head to music.

She is different today. The sunglasses give her distance. For several minutes, as we drive through town—past the gas station where the old Ford's hood is raised, the stores that sell fireworks and apple products—she barely speaks, as if she were just some remote colleague reluctantly giving me a lift somewhere. The back seat of her car, I see, is full of books: Gertrude Stein, Virginia Woolf, Edith Wharton, Flannery O'Connor, Carson McCullers, Harper Lee.

As we get out in the country, though, she begins to talk, to ask questions about the highway. I tell her its story as we return east, to Middleburg.

"This route," I say, "goes back to George Washington. In the 1780s, he envisioned an all-Virginia trade route over the Alleghenies, into the West. That road, the Northwestern Turnpike, started here in Winchester and ended in Parkersburg, on the Ohio. America's Main Street. That was one of its nicknames."

"I like that."

"It wasn't unique, though. The National Road, the first route to the West, was nicknamed the same thing. Later, they called Route 66 the Main Street of America."

"When did it become Highway 50?"

"The U.S. routes came along in 1926," I say. "Originally just as a numbering system, not a highway-building program. It was an early goal of the U.S. government to unite the disparate parts of this whole country. And nothing furthered that more than the establishment of a widespread highway system, linking roads coast to coast with a single route number. That's how the U.S. highways came about."

Patty smokes intently and then turns the radio on very loud for a few minutes before clicking it off. What she really wants to talk about is going. This journey I am taking.

"I went once," she says. "I spent several months traveling, in Europe. I was by myself the whole time, but I met a lot of people. It was actually the best time of my life, if you want to know the truth. I could never find that kind of freedom again."

"Did you ever go back?"

"No. I wanted to. I planned to. To go back and maybe live over there. But it wouldn't have been the same. That's the trouble. Time adds too much baggage to things."

She falls silent for a while, perhaps thinking about some other time in her life when things were better. The breeze is delicious in the misty morning hillsides.

On the road, every day is a surprise. It begins with a sense of possibility, a feeling that burns off like the morning dew.

"I want you to see Middleburg," Patty says, startling me back to conversation, sliding the radio dial through bursts of rock music before she clicks it off again.

Middleburg, Virginia, is a colonial-era hamlet with stone buildings, cobbled walks and shingle signs. At the only traffic light in town, right on Highway 50, is the Red Fox Inn—America's oldest operating tavern. So we're told. We have breakfast there in a polished wooden dining room with Early American decor. The other patrons are all dressed in riding clothes and talking about a polo tournament. The fireplace flames are reflected in our faceted water glasses and burnished silverware.

"I expect I'll become wealthy eventually," Patty says, as she eats her eggs and muffin. "But I wouldn't live here. I'd find someplace no one's discovered yet."

"Where?"

"Out west probably. To me, that's the whole point. To be different. Is that where you're going?"

"Where?"

"West."

"Eventually."

A highway sign in West Virginia, where the road originally was a turnpike for horses and wagons. Photo by Pam Leppin.

She stares; her eyes stay on mine. "You know? Just find a place?"

After the other table clears we are the only ones in this downstairs dining room, and the waiter, a man of about fifty with dark curly hair and a mustache, comes over.

"You know who was sitting where you are on Tuesday?" he asks.

"Who?"

"Jacqueline Kennedy Onassis."

He steps back for effect and momentarily closes his eyes.

Middleburg is a moneyed town where, the story goes, half of the eight hundred residents are millionaires. Four hundred millionaires, the waiter tells us, and he does a curtsy. Jack Kent Cooke lives here; so does Paul Mellon. We listen and nod. Mellon, he says, recently built a house here for Jackie Onassis. There are others: Robert Duvall, Stacy Keach.

"They're trying very hard to preserve the old rich, you see, to keep out the new rich. It isn't easy. Everybody wants to move here. There's a new townhouse development that a lot of people didn't want to come in. The only thing that'll stop it, you understand, is the recession. No one has money anymore. Plus, now the banks aren't lending to developers."

"You must get some good tips," Patty says.

"Well, no. None of them tip more than fifteen percent. Other than Al Neuharth. The *USA Today* founder? He always leaves me a hundred dollars."

"How about Jackie?"

"Jackie? Fifteen. Jackie's demanding, too. She calls in the morning, says she wants a seven-minute egg and her boots polished. It's just the way she lives. She just expects it. She's very grateful. The other day I saw her in the Safeway."

"Did you?"

"Yes, she was buying some meat. They're pretty much normal people who live here, you know. Same as you or me. They just happen to be rich."

After breakfast, we tip 15 percent and head down the cobbled walk along the highway past handsome stone mansions and perfectly manicured lawns. This segment of Route 50 was originally a pioneer trail, I tell Patty. She smokes. Her long, loping stride keeps her half a step ahead of me. Several times she walks into other people or into street signs or newspaper racks on the sidewalk. The sunlight moves higher up on the sides of the stone shops; the crisp morning air with its early promise of perfection is suddenly gone.

"If I do become wealthy, I'll do something humanitarian with the money," Patty says, talking into the breeze. "In a place like this, I'd be too tempted to do something selfish."

In the countryside, wine has suddenly become a big business. Twenty years ago, there were no wineries here; now there are forty, making Virginia possibly the fifth largest producer in the country (the local vintners claim it's third).

The irony is that Thomas Jefferson envisioned this state as a model of wine production two hundred years ago. His attempt to bring European vines to Virginia never took, though, because of the difference in climate. Wine experts say Virginia is still too hot to produce first-rate wine, but the winery people don't agree.

Patty wants to show me the wineries, and she drives, fast, toward Swedenbourg's on the east side of town. "I like getting half looped in the middle of the day sometimes," she says.

"Not me."

"Just occasionally. If I become rich, I'd probably do it once a week."

She drives these old roads quickly, full of an adolescent sort of confidence. A person who hasn't really chosen herself a lifestyle yet—making her a perfect ally in some ways, a terrible one in others.

When we get down to the farmhouse, old Mr. Swedenbourg is at the window by himself, staring out at his 130 acres of grapes, a look of horror frozen on his face. It is his natural expression. He greets us cordially, leading the way back to a metal room at the rear of the building, where the wine is made.

During the tour, he watches closely whenever Patty and I talk, as if trying to learn something about us. At one point, he asks, "Now, where do you come from?"

"North Carolina," Patty says.

His eyes move to me, as if my answer might be different, and I nod.

"Virginia wines, the grape is special, hmm? California wines are too sweet. Virginia wines are more like European wines."

Swedenbourg laughs when Patty asks why he decided to get into the wine business. We amuse him.

"Well. You need to do something with the land, hmm? It is too valuable. And the government made it easy for us."

He turns toward me.

"For the money, then," I say.

He laughs again. "As you say. For the money."

Swedenbourg graciously takes his time, however, and explains to us in detail the wine-making process, how the grapes outside are harvested in September, then put through the de-stemmer and transferred to the presses, where they become juice. The juice is stored in stainless-steel containers before being pumped into fermenting tanks. Yeasts are added, and the wine is stabilized for three weeks before going into oak barrels for flavor. It ages in the barrels two to four months for Semillon, seven to nine months for Chardonnay and Seyval Blanc.

"The special flavor," Swedenbourg says. "That is where it comes from. Now, which is your favorite wine?" he asks me, and there is a quick and, it seems, derisive snort when I say Chardonnay.

After the tour, he offers to let us sample his wines, one at a time. "In Virginia we have some of the best wines in the country now, hmm?"

"This is the part I like," Patty whispers, and Swedenbourg becomes as attentive as a pet whose name has just been called.

"Yes?" he says. "You want to sample?"

Outside, wind moves sunlight through the new fields of grass and the grape vines. The wine has altered slightly the balance of this Virginia countryside.

Patty drives too fast down a narrow, gravel road alongside stone fences toward the Meredyth Winery, one of the largest in the state.

"So if your old jalopy gets running, you're just going?"

"Eventually."

She lights a cigarette.

"I'd go. I'd like to go with you. You know, that's what I resented about my parents. They stayed in one little town all their lives. They never exposed me to things. They told me what to do and what not to do, and I never understood why. And what happened? I got pregnant when I was seventeen."

Already, I'm tiring of her autobiography, but decide to remain a passive adventurer.

Patty is wearing a sleeveless T-shirt again, and her forearms are full of freckles and down. Her thin-lipped mouth has a determined look as she drives, as if she were concentrating on the road. But clearly she isn't. Several times, she loses control from not paying attention; the car slides off the shoulder, and she has to jerk the steering wheel to get us back on.

"Uh-oh," she says, each time it happens.

On the grounds at Meredyth, she parks beside a green barn. A bell hangs in front, and a sign instructs all visitors to ring.

When we do, nothing happens.

"Hello? Yoo hoo?"

Patty pushes open the door to the barn. Inside it's cool, smelling of stone and wine and wood. There are rows of large barrels and racks of wine bottles, but no people. We wander through the rooms for several minutes, then take the stone stairs down into the basement.

A dark-complexioned, impish woman is conducting a tour: "The fifty-three-gallon oak barrels add a buttery flavor to the wine," she is saying, in a surprisingly deep and authoritative voice. "The barrels come from France, and cost four hundred dollars apiece. They have a lifespan of three years."

Patty holds my hand as we become part of the tour group and does not let go. We walk along that way, a couple. Our guide's enthusiasm for wine seems barely containable; as she speaks, saliva bubbles up out of the corners of her mouth. When she tells us that Virginia is the number-three wine producer in the country, almost everyone in the tour seems surprised and impressed. This ranking (though fictitious) puts everything in perspective for us.

The Virginia wine business changed in 1980, she explains, with state legislation favorable to winemakers. It has been a growing industry since. Meredyth was the first licensed winery in the state, going back to 1972. It now produces two hundred thousand bottles a month.

"Why are these wines unique, though?" Patty asks.

"Well, they're better," our guide says and smiles, as if no other explanation were necessary.

A deeply tanned woman from California is on the tour, and she quickly agrees. "Mais oui."

"How about the New York wines?" Patty asks.

"They produce some very fine wines, but they do not have the same quality grape as the Virginia wine."

Afterward, I buy a bottle of Seyval Blanc, and we go outside into a pleasant afternoon breeze.

Many of the streets in this horse country are unpaved, turn-of-the-century roads. People don't want them paved. There's a sense of peace and safety here, and black-topped roads represent something intrusive. It's the same with diners and skipjacks and highway motels from the fifties—scattered remnants of a different time, reminding us that new ways aren't necessarily better. Everyone from our tour group stands around the picnic table and looks at the hills, at the light in the green fields and in the budding trees.

Later we park in the country and watch the sun disappear on the old Civil War hills as the house lights glow more and more brightly. The land here seems to say: There was nothing wrong with the way things were. Change isn't necessary.

"I'd travel with you," Patty says, "but I don't know what I'd do. I need to find a job."

We sit out there a long time, contemplating the trip, letting darkness in. The air has become calmer. Breezes blow quietly up out of the fields. We can hear them faintly in the leaves.

The Apple Capital

G us explains to me that the old Ford will need another day, possibly two, before she's ready. He rubs his chin gravely and looks at the pavement.

"It's just a question of getting the part," he says. "One they sent didn't fit."

But it doesn't matter. Patty and I return to Middleburg. We have a picnic lunch in the countryside and drink ale at an old stone inn and visit the antique shops east of town. Several times, she talks about the trip west, but always hypothetically. If we go, would we take her car or mine? If we run out of money, would we be able to find jobs? The openings quickly fill: She is thinking about it.

In the morning, I pick up the old Ford. "She's good as new," Gus says. When I return to the motel, the brown Toyota is parked outside my room.

"Good as new, he says," I tell her. "Ready to travel west."

With feigned dejection, it seems, Patty announces that she can't go.

"Why?"

"I'm heading for Florida," she says in a voice I don't recognize. "My uncle suffered a stroke."

"A stroke?"

"This morning. I don't think he's going to make it."

She is too serious again, as she had been the first night I met her in the Rebel Lounge. It's as if she's withdrawing all that had followed. In the bright morning sunlight, she gives me a kiss and writes down a phone number in North Carolina and another in Florida. She's wearing a different sleeveless T-shirt today. "I could meet you somewhere on the road," she says, and we make tentative plans for it. "Kansas, or Colorado, maybe." As she drives off, though, the abruptness of the departure feels a little like the aftermath of a mugging. Standing there in the parking lot of the Tourist City Motel, I realize there is only one thing to do—drive.

Out in the countryside, apple blossoms are everywhere. A sign by the road proclaims Winchester "Apple Capital of the World," and the area's commerce celebrates it. Highway 50 passes the Apple Blossom Mall, the Johnny Appleseed Restaurant, the Apple Orchard Motel. The local radio station's slogan is "From the Apple Capital to the Nation's Capital."

At a gas station near the White House Apple Company, the old Ford fills up on high-octane while an attendant tells me that most of the orchards around here were first planted by Johnny Appleseed.

"I didn't think he came this far south."

"Yes, sir," he says, and his grin hardens. "He did."

That ends the small talk. Back in the car, I offer some wisdom to the old Ford: "Locals love to provide information to those passing through. But don't ask them to elaborate, don't question what they've said. Often their stories are made valid simply through repeated tellings." The old Ford purrs.

As I drive out among the orchards, Patsy Cline sings of heartache and the wind smells of wildflowers. A sign in a front yard reads, "Perhaps today—Jesus may come." I feel a tug, think for a while of Patty, driving south in her cluttered Toyota. I decide that I'll send her a postcard, from some other Main Street along the way. But it's not a resolution that makes me feel better.

A market outside of town advertises fresh local apples. The man working, though, says that it's too early in the season for them.

"Why's the sign up, then?"

"We just keep that sign," he says. "I guess just to save trouble more than anything."

Then, to make amends, he gives me a Red Delicious from the south, which is juicy and good. As I eat it, he tells me a little about apples, talking in an aggravating southern drawl.

"The Stayman," he explains. "That's about the best all-around apple in the world. It's good for everything. And then there's the Golden Delicious—good for eating and good for salads. It won't discolor. That's a good apple you're eating right now."

An apple fanatic. I find myself nodding repeatedly, to be polite.

"Of course, there's a lot of secrets people don't know about apples. Pretty simple things. Like, if you want to keep the flavor, don't store apples in paper bags. Paper will suck the moisture. Store your apples in plastic bags. And keep them away from other foods with strong odors, because apples can take on other flavors. They're very good at that."

When I finish, I thank him and head back out onto Highway 50. Not far up the road there is another store, one that sells more apple products than I ever knew existed: vinegar, butter, cider, syrup, soap.

The clerk is as obliging as the last fellow, a young bushy-haired, happy, fat man. His accent is southern but musical.

"People come here from all over the country," he tells me, and when he grins his cheeks resemble apples. "Apple Capital of the USA, they call it."

"Are people really that interested in apples?"

"I don't know what it is, but there's something about apples that captures people's imaginations. Always has been. Don't see it with any of the other fruit, really. Like they say, without apples you wouldn't have a lot of the great fables."

"Fables?"

"Yes, sir. You know, the famous tales and things always seem to have an apple in them. Start at the beginning. Adam and Eve. Snow White. The Trojan War. Sleeping Beauty." He looks at traffic on Highway 50, thinking, then adds one more: "The William Tell Overture."

"Huh."

"You wouldn't have none of them without apples. And I guess you wouldn't have the law of gravity, either."

He's smiling triumphantly now. "Not a lot of people realize that. Most people don't even know apples are the biggest-selling fruit there is."

Another car pulls up. Pennsylvania tags.

If I want to see the largest apple orchard in the world, he tells me, I should turn around and have a look at what's behind Clifton Arnold's house. "Largest orchard in the Shenandoah Valley." He smiles, and his cheeks turn into giant Red Delicious apples.

I drive back down to Clifton Arnold's red-roofed house on the edge of Winchester to have a look. I park along his drive and stare out at the rolling fields of pink blossoms. After a few minutes, a large man comes out the back door, blinking in the afternoon light, lowers his head and walks across the lawn to ask what it is I want. He seems appeased when I say I'm just admiring his apple orchard.

I soon learn, though, that Clifton Arnold is no more the biggest apple grower in the valley than Winchester is the Apple Capital of the World—or than apples are the biggest-selling fruit in the country. (In fact, they are third, behind oranges and grapes.) But as I first look out behind Arnold's white-frame place, the trees are budding in a nice spring breeze, and I smell traces of apple blossoms in the air. For a moment I'm filled with this inflated sense of the fruit, victim of the conspiracy, this American pastime: signs and stories proclaiming exaggerated significance in out-of-the-way places. Gravity. Adam and Eve.

Clifton Arnold, a sturdy, soft-spoken man, leads me down a shady dirt road. He does not try to sell me on the story of apples. He only wants to talk, as if he doesn't get company very often.

"Used to be, we'd produce two hundred and fifty thousand bushels; now, it's more like one hundred thousand," he says. "We get a lot of flak for that sign in town saying we're the apple capital. I'm not saying it wasn't at one time, but it's been awhile."

"What happened?"

"I think the area just never promoted its apples the way they do out in Washington state. That's the real apple capital."

Sunlight sprays down through the branches as we walk in cool, dappled shadows. Arnold chuckles, explaining how the average person doesn't understand the process of making apples. "It's like anything else, you just see the result, which in this case is piles in the grocery stores.

"Lot of things to deal with out here. Last year," he says, "we lost the whole crop in the spring. That's the biggest concern, freezing out. And insects. You got to spray every week to keep off the insects and sometimes they still get on."

Arnold, fifty-four, came here to work one summer in the early sixties as a picker and never left. Now, on the dirt road behind his house, our own shadows move through those of the trees. The wind is kicking up. Walking the same path that he has walked for twenty-six years, I think again of the highway sign in Ocean City: "Sacramento 3073." We turn around at the end of the road, which rises slightly above five hundred acres of trees.

Walking back to the car, he tells me more, talking about apples as if it's the only thing he knows.

"Going to be a windy night," he says. "Where you heading to?"

"Nowhere. We're just driving." I see him looking at the Ford. "Taking Main Street west."

"Never done that," he says. "How far west?"

"Far as it goes."

We stand for several minutes by the car, looking out into the land of apples.

I thank him for showing me the orchard. But instead of saying good-bye, Clifton Arnold resumes talking, repeating himself, taking deep breaths of the air. "Washington state," he says. "That's the real apple capital of the world. The Virginia market has just never done the type of promotions Washington does, although most East Coast growers are convinced they produce a more flavorful fruit."

"Is it more flavorful?" I ask.

"I don't think there's much of a question about that," he says. "I think anybody'd tell you that."

Water Falls in the Shale

I wait for summer on the side of Cacapon Mountain in eastern West Virginia, where wildflowers are in bloom among the oak and beech and sugar maple. The cabin where I decide to stop for a while has one bedroom. No telephone, radio or television. At night, the cool breezes smell of crabapples and honeysuckle; when the air stills, there is sometimes a faint sound of water falling in the shale, or of deer running. For several days at a time here it rains, and I sit in an old musty chair, reading Emerson or writing in a journal, watching the trees bend in the wind. When it stops or turns to drizzle, box turtles sometimes come out around the cabin.

Several hiking trails, marked by orange and blue spots painted on trees, lead to the top of Cacapon Mountain. As the old Ford rests, her faded blue shell parked beside the cabin, becoming increasingly grimy with sap from the pine trees, I explore the trails. It is the first time I have ever done nothing but watch a season change.

Emerson claimed that the woods could give new life. And for a while, they do. "In the woods," he wrote, "a man casts off his years. In the woods is perpetual youth. Within these plantations of God, a decorum and sanctity reign, a perennial festival is dressed, and the guest sees not how he should tire of them in a thousand years. In the woods we return to reason and faith. There I feel that nothing can befall me in life—no disgrace, no calamity—which nature cannot repair."

Eventually, though, the woods have the opposite effect. Too much time among the trees means too much contemplation, too much opportunity for regret. It was a mistake, leaving behind a life that had been built prudently, block by block. A pattern that can never be reversed. To try to do anything without years of apprenticeship now is to be below deck again on Wade Murphy's oyster boat. It is a grim, confining notion.

To buy groceries and escape these thoughts, I sometimes take the old Ford down to a country market at the bottom of the mountain. The store always has a pleasant smell of fresh fruit, and the owner seems glad each time to see me. The first time I go, he tells a West Virginia joke:

"You know how come Jesus never could've come from West Virginia?"

"Why's that?"

"They couldn't find three wise men and they couldn't find no virgin."

Another time, he asks if I'd like to buy a Confederate flag at half price. I ask him why the Confederate flag is flown in West Virginia, when West Virginia wasn't a Confederate state.

He shrugs, a little defensively, it seems.

"Couldn't tell you," he says. "Attitude. A lot of West Virginians think of themselves as part of the South, not the North."

In lieu of a Confederate flag, he gives me a bumper sticker that says, "If You're Not a Hemorrhoid, Get Off My Ass."

"Take it," he says. "You're a good customer."

After several weeks, I need out of these woods, out of these debilitating thoughts.

When I finally leave, the mountain breezes are warm. There are roadside melon stands on the twisting turns, as well as Dairy Queens and country stores. Highway 50 passes through several old wagon-road hamlets, Northwestern Turnpike towns, pastoral hillside places such as Augusta, where people park to visit the antique shops. But as the road winds higher, West Virginia becomes less accommodating. Cars and tires and used appliances rest permanently in clearings. On steep hillsides, the only structures are body shops and an occasional house trailer. A dingy brick building has this sign: "D&S Restaurant Garage and Auto Parts." In the old Confederate stronghold of Romney, kids hang out in parking lots, at the 7-Eleven, or down at the McDonald's (right beside the house where Stonewall Jackson made his headquarters). Processions of young people drive up and down the main street, Highway 50, leaning out of cars and pickups, yelling at one another and pulling curbside. Young people with nothing to do between now and whenever it is they become adults. Nothing to celebrate but Saturday night.

It's up here, in these remote mountain towns with their old-fashioned and often obscure customs, that the journey turns lonesome and strange.

Pool Tables

P ast Romney, everything feels used up: the woods that have been cleared for timber, the junked cars and rusted appliances that have been dropped beside the highway. Wanting to make contact with someone, I stop at a rickety little lounge and restaurant called Evelyn's. It's on the slope of a mountain, beside a huge hole where shale is mined. The mountain wind, cooling slightly, smells disagreeably moist.

Evelyn's is as dark inside as the parking lot outside. There are four pool tables, two booths and a bar. At one end of the bar, an overweight couple in flannel shirts and jeans are holding each other, whispering. I sit on a stool—it wobbles—and ask the barmaid about the hole in the mountain.

"That?" she puts out a coaster.

"Yeah," I say.

She shrugs.

"That's just the shale pit. I don't know much about it. But that man down there," she nods toward one of the flannel shirts, "he works there." The man turns and looks me up and down. Twice. Traditional mountain greeting. "He says there's more shale in these hills than anyone'll ever need," the waitress says and laughs.

"Is that right?"

"Yes, it is," the man says.

"Mining going all right around here?"

"Well, some's better'n others," he says slowly, as if waiting for my challenge. "Coal's no good. Ruined too many lives." The man turns back to the flannel-shirted woman. She whispers something, her eyes right on mine.

I order a light beer and watch the waitress as she gets it. She's wearing black jeans and a lacy shirt that's a little too tight. After she serves mine, she too drinks, from a bottle of Bud that's on the cash-register counter. Her hair is long and bleached, almost white, and she tosses her head often to throw it over her shoulders.

"So, why's the coal business hurting so bad?" I ask her.

"Changing industry, number one," says the man at the end of the bar, loudly. "Which is something you can't help. Foreign markets, number two, which is something you can. If you had to say what was the matter with this country, that's it plain and simple."

He stands there, his legs spread slightly. His arms seem ready to draw a weapon, perhaps for a gunfight. Figuring anything I say to him might provoke an argument, I keep quiet. Soon, the beer begins to work; the darkness inside the bar closes in. Next to the cash register is a sign with a little wall lamp above it, so customers are able to read: "Stress. The confusion created when one's mind overrules the body's basic desire to choke the living shit out of some asshole who desperately needs it."

"Ever get crowded?" I ask the woman, after several minutes pass.

She shrugs, looks me up and down.

"Couple of nights. Can get right rowdy sometimes. On Saturday nights."

I look out at the darkened lounge area—the jukebox surface glowing back by the restrooms—and wonder what sorts of things go on. Then I realize this is Saturday night.

She shrugs again. "People let their hair down, you know." She's wiping off the counter by the beer cooler now. "You're not from West Virginia, are you?"

"No. How do you know?"

She tosses her hair, this time using her hand for extra effect.

I drink my beer for a while and give up trying to talk. The jukebox is playing something by Gregg Allman called "I'm No Angel." The passive adventurer's lesson: Everywhere you go, you have to pay something—time, experience—to be accepted. The country is made up of millions of cliques, social solar systems, secret societies.

After a few minutes, a group of four men and one woman comes in. They go to the back, to the farthest pool table from the bar, and begin setting up. One of the men comes up to the bar and orders, nodding a cool, suspicious hello to me. To the barmaid he says something quickly. It sounds like, "Dawny, see that Ace over town's back in?"

"Who?"

"Pete's cousin."

"Oh, yeah. I told you."

"B and E man," he says, and they both roar with laughter.

"Can't say we didn't try."

"Same story."

"I tell you what. Lester'd be there. But he said no more of it."

"That'll get it."

"I'm telling you."

They're grinning as they turn away. He carries the drinks back on a tray. All beers.

The game is pocket billiards. The man's name is Ernie. He wins two games and points a cue stick at me.

"Ready, captain?"

"Nah."

"Come on, chief," he says, racking the balls. "Playing winners."

He doesn't offer another chance to say no, so we play. He lets me break, and I sink one. The next shot I miss. Ernie, who is tall, slender and bearded, goes on a run.

Final score: 14–1.

"All right," Ernie says, chalking up.

Afterward, I sit at a table and watch, humbly, and drink. He plays the woman, who is tall and gangly. As the game goes on, one of the men tells me a story about a deer hunt back in eighty-three, which ended tragically. "When you get into them hills down there," he says, "it's easy to lose track of your position. Bullet went right through my uncle's heart. And this man tells me the minute he pulled the trigger that he knew it wasn't no deer. But by that time he knows it's too late. There's nothing to do."

"Shit," says another man.

The conversation lags, and I ask about accommodations. "Is there a motel nearby?"

"How many hours you want it for, chief?" Ernie asks.

They all snicker.

"Overnight."

"Yeah? Try just up the road, there's three of 'em," he says. "Close up pretty early, though."

"The two major sports up here, you know what they are?" asks the man who hasn't spoken.

I shake my head. He stares until I look away.

"Hunting and adultery."

Again, laughter.

"You know why Jesus didn't come from West Virginia?" the man whose uncle was shot asks me. "They couldn't find three wise men and they couldn't find no virgin." He laughs loudly at the joke. I politely join in.

Several miles ahead, the mountain road crosses water on an old metal bridge. I stop at a place called the Nod Wink Motel, which is more or less across the street from another lounge called the Shotgun Tavern. There are four pool tables in the Shotgun too, and only one is being used. I count ten people watching the game, which, I'm surprised to see, is between Ernie and the man whose uncle was shot.

I go up to order. Ernie leans on his cue.

"Get your motel room, Eric?" he asks, and for some reason it provokes laughter.

"Got it," I say.

"You're driving a Ford, captain, better be careful," he says. "They don't make Ford transmissions for hills like this. Go look at the graveyard up near Romney."

I stand at the bar for a while, wondering if he means an auto graveyard or a real one. I think of the old Ford ending up in a junk car lot on a West Virginia hillside. One of the four women at a table opposite mine—husky, masculine-looking—plays Ernie in what turns out to be a very close match. Another puts money in the jukebox, and the three of them sit and watch. They're dressed in short pants and white T-shirts. Two sing along as "I Want Your Sex" plays.

The game is, again, winners, and by invitation I play one but don't win. Mary, the masculine girl, in her second try, does, beating Ernie and then another man. Ernie stands back by the bar and keeps teasing her about being afraid to give him a rematch.

More people come in, including a woman with a beehive hairdo, a Dwight Eisenhower look-alike in tow. Rolled up in a sleeve of Ike's bright blue T-shirt is a pack of Marlboros. Ernie is worked up, dancing to the music. He saunters over to the couple, flirts, puts his arm around the woman's shoulder and whispers something. Eisenhower shows no expression but watches intently.

A blond-haired woman comes over to my table and introduces herself as Pearl. We shake hands. "Where you from?" she asks.

I tell her.

"I've been there."

"Have you?"

"There or Virginia Beach."

"There's a big difference."

We talk for a while. She says she reads palms and wouldn't mind seeing my lifeline. I show her. She rubs her finger up and down my palm, then holds hands for a moment.

"You like it here?" I ask.

"I don't mind it much, neither. It's okay. We get to go rafting sometimes. Down on Cheat. I don't mind it."

After a few minutes, she surprises me by asking, a little nervously, "You want to buy any smoke?"

"Pardon?"

Her eyelashes flutter, her skin flushes.

"He wants to know if you want to buy some smoke."

"No, thanks."

"Okay."

Embarrassed, she goes back to looking at my lifeline, but too self-consciously. It makes us both uncomfortable.

In the men's room here there's a "Dixie Deluxe" prophylactic machine ("nationally advertised") and a sticker that reads "The Ku Klux Klan Is Watching You—Fight For White Rights." When I come out of the bathroom, Pearl is back at the bar, talking to Ernie, who has his arm around her. I watch the billiards and drink a while longer.

The four women get up to go—maybe to Evelyn's, where the crowds ought to be "right rowdy" by now. "Good game," Ernie says faintly as they leave. Mary smiles, without acknowledging him.

When I finally leave, the door opens behind me. Pearl. "Don't go yet," she says. "We're just starting to have fun." I'm tired, though, and thinking about the clean motel linens. The mountain air is filled with fireflies, the land lit by a full moon.

"Pretty night," she says. "Where are you staying?"

"Right over there."

"Convenient."

We stare at each other for a few moments in the honeysuckle-scented breeze. "Maybe I'll come over later and we can smoke a joint," she says in a teasing way and abruptly goes back in.

King Coal

C oal Is King" reads a faded bumper sticker on a pickup in the shale hills near Mount Storm, West Virginia. Faded pride. Along a thin gravel road crowded with leafy oaks and yellow poplars, women and children sit on the porches of old wooden houses and watch as I drive by. No one waves. In the hot overgrown yards are rusted cars, pieces of furniture. Ore-rich rivers spill down the mountainsides, silver and orange in the twisting sunlight, and the shadowy air buzzes with insects. Downhill, a boy holding a dead squirrel by the tail walks in the center of the road, and I have no choice but to stay behind him all the way, until he gets to his house. There he stands by the mailbox and, turning, grins at me.

The old Ford's red light goes on in these hills, and she begins making a chuck-chuck sound; her response, perhaps, to such a recalcitrant land. Near Oakland, I stop by the gates of a coal mine and lift the hood to have a look.

A silver-haired man with craggy features appears in the doorway of the main building, and again I feel like a trespasser. He nods, not at me but at the engine.

"Carburetor adjustment," he says.

"Is that what it is?"

He reaches down and fiddles. In less than a minute, he has fixed it.

"Not here looking for work, I hope," he says, as he pulls out a pack of Winstons. He grins, like it's a joke. Behind him towers a five-story-tall mountain of coal.

"Don't have any?"

"Well, no, nothing underground, anyway. May have something topside."

Coal, he says, as we stand in the hot air watching the miners come up from underground, was once all anybody talked about around here. It was all anybody did. King Coal, they called it. But for three decades, the mines in these mountains have been going out of business.

"Can't compete with all the Third World countries," the man, Brian Allison, says. "Can't do anything about the nuclear power market. This mine opened in 1977, during the energy crisis. It employs three hundred fifteen. But its lifespan is less than twenty years, and there's no more land available to extend that. Nothing you can do.

"You mine the coal from the earth and then it's gone. That's how it works. Then you look elsewhere," Allison says. "A lot of people who've lost their jobs, who aren't engineers, feel like they're stuck. A lot of them stay up here in the mountains."

"What's the job that's available topside?" I ask. The idea of working for a while in a coal mine, of infiltrating this bleak, uninviting mountain country, suddenly appeals to me.

He takes my question seriously. "Let me call Joe. He can show you. There's one shift available, I think."

Allison, the head engineer, invites me into the main building, a brick-and-tile box resembling a schoolhouse. As we wait for Joe, he tells me more about coal, and about himself, about the event that colored his childhood.

When he was seven, Allison says, his father was killed in a mining accident. "A locomotive engine fell on him. In Kentucky. I grew up thinking that whatever I did with myself was okay, so long as it wasn't in coal mining. But I grew up in a mining town in Tennessee and was always associated with people who worked in the mines. When the job's there and the money's there, it's sometimes hard to get away from it. So when I came out of the service I figured I'd take a job in the mine because the money was good. And after a while I enjoyed it. It's something that just gets in the blood."

He takes deep drags on the cigarette, smoking until only the filter is left. One more man living a life he didn't want, yet accepting it. When you stay in one place, life can close in around you, force acceptance.

"What happens when the mine closes? Are three hundred fifteen people going to be out of work?"

"Yep. It's happened several times in the past ten years. A lot of the people who've lost their jobs don't know what else to do, so they stay in these hills. Those are the ones you feel sorry for."

"What else is there?"

"Lumbering. That's bigger than coal. And farming. Some say tourism, but that's more of a wish than a reality."

It's a still, hot day; there's a faint smell of flowers and honeysuckle through the opened windows.

"I figured if I was going to be a miner, I was going to be a good one," Allison says. "I didn't want to spend the rest of my life underground, like some folks have. Or spend ten years in the mines and find myself out of work. I wanted to understand the industry. So I went to school at the University of Kentucky and I studied to be an engineer. 'Course, it's changed a lot. Twenty years ago it was hard physical labor working in the mines. Now the work is all done by radio-controlled or hydraulically controlled machines."

As we talk, the sun drops, glaring briefly in the leaves. Allison surprises and impresses me. A man who has risen above the oppressive economic smog of these hills and done things right. Someone to learn from.

When Joe, a much younger man with dark hair and a mustache, arrives, Allison introduces me as "the fellow interested in the tower job."

Without saying anything, Joe hands me a hard hat and leads me outside to his Chevy truck. I sense, in his silence, disapproval.

"Ever work in the mines before?" he says as we pull out.

"Nope."

"Brian's putting you topside?"

"Apparently."

"It's a temporary job. A part-time thing. Ever work with machinery?"

"Not in years," I say.

As we drive downhill along a narrow gravel road, Joe waves at passing pickups and says things that I don't catch and some I do. There are actually three mines here, he tells me, on five thousand acres of land.

"After we use that up, that's it, they're going to close it. Going to make everything worse around here than it already is."

"What'll you do when that happens?" I ask, as we glide past a clearing where there are junk cars and heaps of tires.

"I'm in engineering," he eventually answers. "So I can be transferred. Most of the other people will just be out of work. It's rough living here."

We drive past the entrance to one of the mines, and Joe points to the conveyer belts that move the coal—three and a half miles of belts on the surface, twenty miles underground.

I ask him about health concerns.

"It's the coal dust we hear about most. We've been doing what we can to improve it. Hot day in summer, though, ain't much you can do. Today's unusually hot and there ain't much you can do. Most people're just happy to have a job."

Finally, we come to the train tower. "This is where the job is," he says, parking the truck. "It's loading the steam coal from stockpiles onto Penn Electric train cars. That sound like fun?"

Upstairs, a man whose face and clothes are covered with coal dust stares as he is introduced to me. A minstrel singer in blackface.

"It's dirty work," Joe says, and the other man's face creases in a smile.

"Ain't so bad you can't get used to it."

"Mostly it's just tedious," Joe offers.

As Joe looks on, the other man, Rick, explains the responsibilities of the "tower job." He pulls one lever and coal pours down a chute into a train car. When the car is full, he pulls another lever, and the train moves forward until the next empty car is in place.

"Almost eighteen hundred tons of coal an hour can be loaded this way," Joe says. "We send out a train every day all year round. In winter, we have to mix antifreeze in with it."

"Where does it all go to?"

"Morgantown. Electric company."

I spend the rest of the sweltering afternoon up there in the tower with Rick, learning when to pull the first lever and when to pull the second. It reminds me of the tedium of oystering. Men doing a machine's work.

At five o'clock, Rick offers to drive me back to the main building, where the old Ford is sitting patiently, her windows coated with a fine black film. I go in to see Allison.

"How did it go?" he asks.

"Seemed simple enough."

"It's simple, sure, but it's work. It's a long day's work."

He lets me fill out an application and asks my plans. "You looking to settle up here?"

I shrug. There's a strong urge to find something stable again, to do an honest day's work, and I tell him yes.

"It's a temporary job," he says. "How temporary depends."

"Okay."

The tug: finding a new life in such a seemingly resistant land. Allison asks if I can be back the next morning.

I drive up the road under a darkening sky and find a motel room near Mount Storm at a little past nine. The proprietor, a tiny old white-haired woman, seems wary of me.

"Do you have any identification?" she asks after I fill out the registration form.

"Identification?"

She studies my driver's license for far too long, standing behind the huge counter in the motel office, her dentures making funny clicking sounds. Before handing it back, she looks at the reverse side as if she might find something there to disqualify me.

"Just one night?" she asks.

"For starters," I reply.

Her lip curls with disdain. She puts me in the farthest room from the office and watches from the doorway as I walk to it.

For seven days I drive nine miles to Oakland and sit up in the train tower, sometimes with Rick, sometimes by myself, pulling levers and sweating. It is gratifying, at first, to do a real job again. I grow comfortable with the feel of the levers, the familiar sound of the trains' brake shoes. At night, I come home looking like a black man, and take a long, hot shower in the motel room.

Some days the old woman has been in the room to make the bed and change the towels, some days not. One night I see that she has been in my notebooks and left one of them open on the bureau. The second time it happens I walk over to the office and knock several times. There's no answer. As I turn to walk away, the door opens slightly. It's still latched.

"Oh," I say, trying to be polite. "I just wanted to request that no one goes in the room. I don't need the linen changed daily."

The door slams.

A half hour later, a large middle-aged man with baggy eyes and pock-marked skin knocks at my door. He positions himself so he can jam a leg in if necessary.

"What's your problem, bub?" he says, and I see that his teeth are as yellow as his T-shirt.

I shake my head. "No problem."

"No? Well, when anybody accuses my mother of stealing, he's got a problem. My mother wouldn't steal nothing from nobody. You understand me, bub? We're not that kind of people."

I try to explain to him that I didn't accuse her of stealing, but he doesn't hear a word of it. He stands with his arms at his sides like he's readying to charge at me.

"It's a misunderstanding," I say. "I certainly didn't accuse her of stealing."

"Well, if I hear you giving her any more trouble, I'll make sure you don't stay in this area another day. You understand me, bub?"

In the train tower, Rick says whatever's on his mind. Mostly, it's about the economy. Or politics, or how the Cincinnati Reds are doing. And every day there's a comment about the amount of mustard his wife put in that day's bologna sandwich, as well as a critique of the previous night's TV. Often, he groans about the heat. It's the worst heat wave in twenty-three years, I hear on the news.

Coming off work, I usually stop to talk with Allison, to learn about the business, to absorb his simple wisdom. "Are you happy?" he asks one afternoon. "Don't forget to ask yourself that. If the answer's no, then you ask yourself another question: Why not?"

In the evenings, I write in my journal or have a few drinks down the road at the Mountaintop Bar. Some nights Rick comes in and sits with me, saying whatever is on his mind.

I feel so at home driving these mountain roads that I even think about staying. Rick says he can get me a good deal on a house if I want. A small, wood-frame, he says, by a stream.

I am completely unprepared when, the next night, a man comes over to me at the Mountaintop and asks, "So what's the deal, pal? What makes you think you can come up here and take one of our jobs away from us?"

I stare back at him, and he stares me down.

"I didn't think of it that way."

"Well, I do." He goes back across the bar but looks over again several times. The question, the directness of his eyes, makes me realize that I'm no longer welcome.

Maybe it's only coincidence, but the next morning one of the old Ford's tires is flat. As I put on a spare, the little woman watches from the office window. That's the day I tell Allison I'm quitting.

The Most Famous Dairy Queen

On a winding stretch of George Washington's Highway, as this segment of Route 50 is now called, I come to the most famous Dairy Queen in West Virginia. "Home of Retire the Penny USA," reads the sign out front. This is the Dairy Queen that will not accept pennies, and the stooped, wrinkled woman working today tells me why, after I order a hot fudge.

"It's the same idea the rest of the country's going to come to eventually, that a penny ain't worth nothing no more. It ain't worth the fuss."

"It's worth one cent."

"Yeah, but one cent ain't worth nothing. Ain't worth the fuss. Used to be you could buy candy for a penny. Now it costs a quarter."

A sign by the window explains just how the Aurora Dairy Queen's policy about pennies works, including examples:

"41 to 42 will be charged 40 cents

43 to 44 will be charged 45 cents

46 to 47 will be charged 45 cents

48 to 49 will be charged 50 cents"

At the bottom of the sign, some humor: "Come to Your Cent-ses. I've Lost Mine, Use Yours."

"Ever get any complaints about it?" I ask the woman.

"Nope, everybody seems pretty relieved, to tell you the truth. The whole country's heading toward the same thing. Pretty soon no one's going to accept pennies. It ain't worth the fuss."

Retire the Penny is the idea of Don Crumbaker, who owns the Aurora Dairy Queen and lives part of the year in a trailer behind it. I eat my sundae on a rock in the warm, thin mountain breeze, listening to Crumbaker, sixty-two, proudly talk about his Retire the Penny campaign and all the publicity it has received, locally and nationally.

"It's overwhelmed me," he says. "I didn't expect it. But I'll tell you, there wouldn't be this kind of interest if we weren't on to something."

"Where did the idea come from?"

"Well. I'll tell you. The closest bank here is fifteen miles. I bought this Dairy Queen three years ago, and it didn't take long for me to realize it was a lot of trouble to make all those trips to the bank over a bunch of pennies. People were in agreement with me. They don't want to have to deal with all those pennies."

In the spring, a story about Crumbaker went out over the Associated Press wire, he says, and the penny campaign quickly became political. A countermovement, called "Save the Penny," was started.

Crumbaker snorts at it. "It was supposed to sound like an All-America thing. But I investigated. It was actually the zinc lobby out of Tennessee. See, as soon as anything gets going, the lobbyists come along and work against it. The lobbyists and pollsters, that's who runs this country.

"But, I'll tell you, everyone's in agreement with me. On Route 50, we have every state in the union go by. States I've never been to before, like the Dakotas. And I'm always saying to people, 'What are you doing out here?' It usually turns out they're here for the recreation. A lot of them have kayaks and things. But no matter where they're from, they tell me how glad they are I've started this. People don't want pennies anymore. That's just a fact.

"The government thinks it's a threat to the sales tax. Well," he chuckles softly, "it isn't that. Inflation just keeps lowering what a penny's worth. It'll be gone in ten years, anyway, just based on inflation. If it costs more to make a coin than it's worth, they can't mint it anymore. That's law."

More mountain wisdom. Insects buzz in the tall weeds as we sit there. The sundae has mostly melted.

"Of course, you see a lot of stores now with those little cups by the cash registers so you don't have to use pennies. People don't want them anymore, but they keep making them because of the lobbyists. That's the only reason. Did you know that seventy-five percent of all coins are pennies? Fourteen billion pennies are minted a year, and they're not worth anything." He shakes his head in a very slow, satisfied way.

Twenty stores have already adopted Crumbaker's Retire the Penny campaign, he says. "I made up some T-shirts and hats and people wanted to buy them. I didn't expect that. It's just one of those things that the people agree on, but the government is keeping it from happening. So you have to do it yourself."

Ahead, the road tilts steeply uphill. There are other stopping points. Down a hillside near Aurora, for example, is a stone house with a shingle sign announcing the Red Horse Tavern. In the adjacent field, there's an old Conestoga wagon. Once, this house was a major stopping point on Washington's turnpike for wagons and mule teams headed west to the Ohio Valley. A man named Bob Guthrie is restoring the house on the day I stop, and he gives me a tour. "This was one of the roughest roads in the country," he says. "The Northwestern Turnpike was a road they didn't really want to build, but they had to. When people reached here and saw this inn, they were ready to stop. Didn't matter if they had to sleep five or six to a bed." Guthrie drinks several Stroh's beers from a pewter mug as he talks about the Northwestern Turnpike.

Several miles away, at Cool Springs Park, a waterwheel turns among the trees, marking the spot, supposedly, where Washington camped when he was surveying the area for his road.

"Fallen Rock," one sign says. "Falling Rock," another.

Later, by a waterfall next to the winding two-lane highway, I pull off and decide to sleep out the misty night in the old Ford. To take the treacherous mountain turns with fresh eyes.

Shrine in a Railroad Town

T he first Union soldier killed by Confederates is buried in Grafton, West Virginia, on the first terrace of the National Cemetery. Thornesberry Bailey Brown. Shot with a musketball through the heart near a B&O Railroad bridge on May 22, 1861.

After visiting the cemetery, I drive into downtown Grafton and stop at the laundromat. Two weeks' worth of clothes need cleaning again. There are several old men and one younger man sitting on chairs in front of the machines, although only one of the other washers is in use. They're all drinking coffee and watching the road, barely noticing when I come in.

Several times, as my washer churns, I try to strike up a conversation, to ask these men about Grafton.

"Nothing notable about this town," says one of the fellows, a bald man whose old white shirt is buttoned wrong. "Nothing worth talking about."

"What happened is the railroad's gone," says another. "It's nothing more complicated than that." His hand is shaking slightly on the coffee cup.

"I guess it's the story of a lot of towns."

"Some," he says, looking out at the street. "Each town's different. Few places as bad as this one."

"This one's lost the glass companies, the pottery companies, the railroad," says the younger man, who looks like he might be the bald man's son. "We only got a couple of things left. We got the company that makes those flaps that go over the tires of tractor-trailer trucks."

"There've been all sorts of plans for making this a booming little town again. But it can't work."

"Why?"

"They ain't got the money to do it, first of all. And even if they did, nobody'd come here anyway. You can't do it without the industry. And nobody wants to bring industry to a place as god-awful as this little town." The men all laugh at this, though it sounds like they're coughing.

"It's the malls now is what people want," the younger man says. "We got the malls not too far away. So nobody's going to come to Grafton to shop."

"Is the railroad gone completely?"

"It's mostly gone, let's say. Used to be sixty, seventy percent of the people in Grafton worked for the railroad. Now it's gone and nothing's come along to replace it. Doesn't look like nothing will. This is just sort of an old useless mountain town."

"Towns can run out of their usefulness, just like people," the bald man says.

What they fail to say for a long time at the Grafton laundromat is that right down the street is the little church that gave birth to the international Mother's Day holiday.

When the men finally tell me, it sounds improbable: Mother's Day would not have had its origins in a grim, brick railroad town like this, I think. Surely, there would be signs along the highway promoting it. But after my clothes are dried and stacked in the front seat of the old Ford, I walk over to the two-story, red-brick church building, and Leonora Shafer, who works there, tells me it's true.

Shafer has a different slant on Grafton than the men in the laundromat: "This has become a retirement community, now that the railroad's gone, and we kind of like that. It's a peaceful town. Didn't used to be that way, of course. There's a lot more we could do with Grafton. Like Mother's Day. We could promote that a little better, I guess. But a lot of us like Grafton as a quiet little town, after living here through the railroad years."

It was Anna Jarvis's daughter who proposed, in 1908, to the church superintendent that a Mother's Day holiday be celebrated in Grafton. The date picked was the third Sunday in May, the anniversary of her mother's death. Two years later, a state Mother's Day proclamation was issued, and in 1914 a national resolution was passed. Within a few years, Mother's Day had become an international holiday, celebrated on or near the date of Anna Jarvis's death.

Shafer works at the Mother's Day shrine for two dollars a day now "because it's an important part of the community." I'm the only visitor today, and she gives me a lengthy tour of the building, showing the room where the first Mother's Day was celebrated and then the chamber where Mrs. Jarvis taught her Sunday School class. She leads me upstairs, to the shrine itself. Beside the altar is a sundial that John Glenn's mother donated to the church in 1962, the year her son orbited the earth. On the walls are murals depicting biblical scenes.

"The church holds services only one day a year now," she says. "On Mother's Day. The rest of the year it's just open for tours, like this."

"Get many visitors?"

"We do pretty well," she says. "Well, no, not as well as we could. Mostly because not a whole lot of people know we're here. The origins of things get forgotten."

Outside, it's hot, breezy and overcast. Clouds are thick through the trees above the brick storefronts. A man is sleeping on the sidewalk in front of Capri Pizza as I come out into the late afternoon from the Mother's Day shrine. In the hills, there's a pleasant smell of foliage, of meals cooking.

By Bridgeport, the land has flattened. "More normal times are ahead," I assure the old Ford, as we pull to a stop in front of a place called "Exciting Irene's Fast Foods." I wonder, going in, if it's Irene or the fast food that's exciting. Obviously not the restaurant.

The waitress comes over. She asks, "What y'all wanta order?"

"Coke," I say.

"Nothin' else?"

"Nope."

She takes the menu and does not speak to me again. The two men eating Exciting Irene's hamburgers are talking about Coffindaffer's crosses. I'd noticed them: sets of three crosses on the West Virginia hillsides, one cross yellow, two blue. A wealthy retired businessman named Bernard Coffindaffer began putting

Coffindaffer's crosses. Made of telephone poles, there are now more than five hundred sets of them in the country, seen by ten million motorists each year. The first ones went up in West Virginia towns with biblical names.

the crosses up in 1985, starting here in West Virginia, and no one has been able to stop him. There are five hundred sets of them now, all over the country.

"That's America," one of the men says. "Get enough money, you can do any goddamn thing you want to do, no matter how screwy it is."

"I don't see anything screwy about spreading the word. That's Coffindaffer's mission, and I say more power to him. I think the man's sincere in what he's doing."

"Shit. You want to spend three million dollars, you ought to build a hospital. Or feed the poor in Africa. Not put up fucking crosses and have people write newspaper stories about you."

"Hell, you accomplish a lot more making people think about their religion than having them pay money to some charity."

"Those things don't make people think about their religion, they make 'em think about Coffindaffer."

So it goes. There is no resolution in sight when I leave Exciting Irene's and head west again.

Nearby is the industrial city of Clarksburg, named for explorer George Rogers Clark, at the confluence of the Elk River and the west fork of the Monongahela. Then Parkersburg, on the Ohio, another broken brick city, the western end of Washington's Northwestern Turnpike.

Parkersburg was named for Alexander Parker, who bought 1,350 acres here in 1783. It was the turnpike that brought people through, that built up Parkersburg. Today, though, many of the buildings in the downtown section are boarded up. Others have been turned into adult book and video stores. Homeless men watch from the sidewalks as I pass.

I've had my fill of West Virginia, I decide, and cross over the Ohio into another state before stopping for the night. *Ohio:* Iroquoian Indian name, meaning "fine river." No longer on the route of Washington's turnpike, Highway 50 follows the course of the old Ohio Trail, an Indian warpath used to intercept travelers on the river. I camp beside the water with a new sense of beginning. A new day, a new state. Another chance to start over.

American Painter

After West Virginia, I reach the pleasant, hilly farm country of eastern Ohio, where dairy cows graze by the two-lane highway, where the corn is green and tall and where many of the barns have "Chew Mail Pouch Tobacco" display-painted on them. I hear several stories about the barns, all of them passed along with great authority but contradicting one another.

A feed store operator near Athens tells me that most of the barns were painted in the 1930s and that the Mail Pouch company has been out of business since about 1955. "They'll all be gone, probably, in another few years," he says sadly. But this can't be true, because some of the signs I pass seem freshly painted.

A tractor salesman in McArthur guffaws at this first story, then digs his hands into his overall pockets and changes his style of laughter: "Hee hee hee hee."

"No, you must be talking to the wrong people to get a story like that," he says. "It's actually a family of five or six brothers that do all the barn painting, and they do it all during April."

"Why April?"

"Well, apparently that's the time the company lets them do it. Every April, they go around. I imagine the climate has something to do with it. And then, that's your tourism season too."

"What are the brothers' names?"

"I think it's the Bloch brothers."

Not far from Albany, I stop at a service station and an attendant shakes his head slowly at the story of the six brothers.

"The signs is all painted by one man," he says, "if you want to know the truth."

"One man?" I say, anticipating a punch line.

"Harley Warrick. He lives up in Belmont. Hillbilly. Some people say he's got a moonshine operation up there too."

Thinking that there is perhaps some running joke about the Mail Pouch signs, I smile at this man but decide to take a detour north to Belmont, nevertheless, to see what I can find.

It rains as I drive north, but by the time I reach the Belmont exit the sun is bright again, and there's a fresh steamy smell to the cornfields. At the Belmont gas station, two men in overalls are sitting in chairs looking out the window. Traditional small-town pastime. I ask if they know where Harley Warrick lives.

"Sure do," says one of them. "Just follow the road all the way through town and then make a left at the big red barn."

"Okay."

"Take it out of gear and coast down to the bottom of the hill, then go up the gravel road right by the red barn. If you start going uphill again and you ain't on the gravel, then you've gone too far. Got that?"

I tell him I do, although I miss the turn the first time—mostly because all of the barns here are red. The gravel road up to Warrick's house is alarmingly narrow and tilts at about a forty-five-degree angle. At the top is a large house and several trees with bird feeders in them. I look closely and see that the bird feeders are miniature barns, with "Chew Mail Pouch Tobacco" painted on the sides.

A little man in overalls comes to the doorway of a real barn beside the house and frowns.

"Harley Warrick?"

He looks at me, puffing on his pipe.

"You with the EPA?"

"No."

He gives me a good looking-over.

"Okay," he says. "Then who are you?"

I explain to him the different stories I had heard about the signs. I tell him I wanted to find out which was for real.

He chuckles. "Well, it's only me," he says. "I do all the Mail Pouch barns. There ain't no team."

"No brothers?"

"Nope."

It's beginning to drizzle again, and Harley invites me to his workshop inside the old barn.

"The government recently banned high-sulfur coal burning,"

he says, leading me to the back, where he's constructing Mail Pouch bird feeders, "and it's put people here out of work. Things are bad enough anyway. The timber industry is failing, the glassworks business got knocked out by China. There ain't much of nothing left around here."

"I've heard that elsewhere."

"So if you was with the EPA, you wouldn't be too popular around here right now. People had about enough of government around these parts."

Since 1970, Harley Warrick has been the lone painter of Mail Pouch advertisements, carrying on a tradition that goes back about a hundred years. As signs and billboards came along early in the century, most American businesses stopped barn advertising. But Mail Pouch never did. Now the barns are considered Americana.

Harley Warrick, the sole painter of Mail Pouch signs on barns, Belmont, Ohio.

"It goes back to when Lady Bird Johnson passed that Beautification Act, and they tried to outlaw painting on the barns. That's one thing you can't do. That's when the interest really started. It's just the nature of American people. Whenever you try to tell them they can't do something, that's when it picks up popularity."

The drizzle has turned again to a soft summer rain, beating gently on the roof of the barn. As Warrick speaks, his eyes seem to look at you with the sagacity of another time.

Years ago, he says, "you knocked yourself out to get people to let you paint a sign on their barn. Now we get more offers than we can accommodate. Nowadays they pay us. And you know what? I ain't doing anything different than I was doing forty years ago."

"What does that mean?"

"Well, I'm not a psychologist, but I think it means plenty. I think people have been rushing forward so much that all at once they figure it's time to back up a little."

He relights his pipe, a lengthy, satisfying ritual.

"It's like a guy overdrives himself. That's the way we've been moving. Everyone's always looking for the next modern thing. Well, hell, Mail Pouch decided to stay where they were at. We didn't do anything different. The sign's exactly the same as it was forty years ago. We don't change the colors or nothing. And then all at once, everyone came around and got interested in what we were doing."

These are the old traditions of Main Street, I think, like the unpaved roads of Middleburg, the twenty-four-hour diners, the corner pharmacies.

"It's gotten so out of hand," Warrick says, "that some people are calling what I do modern art. That should tell you something's not right."

He stuffs more tobacco in his pipe and lights it again. He puffs several times.

"'Course nowadays they call just about anything art. Piss in a bottle, that's art. Nowadays, you have to have a thousand words to explain a picture. Someone like Andrew Wyeth or Norman Rockwell, one picture is worth a thousand words. To me, if it doesn't tell a story when I first look at it I don't want to keep looking at it. There's too many goddamn intellects. I think that's what's wrong with this country. Too many intellects, nobody to do the work."

Warrick grew up on Highway 50 in Londonderry, near Chillicothe. When he began painting barns in the forties, there were four crews working for the Bloch Brothers Company of Wheeling, West Virginia. Now it's just him. He paints or repaints about twenty barns a week these days in a nine-state area composed of Pennsylvania, West Virginia, Ohio, western Maryland, Kentucky, Indiana, New York, Illinois and Michigan. Harley usually goes out for a week at a time in his pickup truck, staying in motels in the nine-state area.

"I'm always home Friday evenings for the stock car races," he says. "I get my work done by Friday, the way it should be."

All of the barn painting is done freehand, he says. There are no stencils, no measuring tools. Every once in a while, he says, he'll put three c's in tobacco just to see if anyone notices.

Outside, the sky turns to twilight, then silvery night, as the rain pours, its cool smell coming in the opened barn doors. Warrick, like many of the people I've met on this journey, obviously enjoys having an audience. He is in no hurry for me to go.

"When you really look at it," he says, "most of this stuff they call 'progress' ain't really progress at all. I think people are finally starting to give up on 'progress' and get back to things that really work. People are starting to realize that you can't do things the easy way. That it just doesn't work."

He reminds me, as he says this, of Wade Murphy, the oysterman. Doing the same thing over and over. Deeply believing that there is no other way that works as well. When he asks me to consider coming out with him sometime to learn barn painting, I balk: I'd just as soon work for Murphy.

When I leave Warrick's workshop, it's nearly nine, and the rain is heavy. He walks to the car, tells me to be careful going back down the hill.

"Where are you driving to?"

"I'm driving west on Highway 50."

"Good highway. Got a lot of barns out alongside it. How far you expect to get tonight?"

"Not sure."

He nods, reaching for the pipe.

"Same way I am. Not sure where I'm going a lot of times until I get out on that highway."

It takes nearly ten minutes before I reach the bottom of Harley Warrick's hill again. Then it's an easy drive back to Highway 50.

The Only Truly American Sport

I t's in the overgrown hill country near Stewart, Ohio—where I camp beside a wide but shallow stream—that I learn the difference between a wedge car and a jig. In this land of dairy farms and cornfields, where the cicadas hum incessantly, it is an important distinction. On summer weekends, what people do here is go to the stock car races, some to watch, some to drive. It is the favorite activity of these hill folks who during the week cut timber, mine coal, repair cars. "You're always surprised to see what they look like when they step out of the race car," says the manager of the campground where I stay.

The cars begin appearing at about six o'clock every Friday and Saturday, towed on trailers behind pickups headed along farm roads toward the track. I follow them deep into the lush countryside; there are no signs. Eventually—even before the grandstand appears—engines sound like faraway thunder and the breeze carries a smell of gasoline.

The cars are roaring through their practice laps when I arrive, preparing for tonight's special race, the Mark Balzano Classic. I find a seat in the regular section of the grandstand, and buy a can of Budweiser for a dollar from a largely toothless man. The other part of the grandstand is the "No Beer" section.

"You come up from Parkersburg?" he asks, shaking beer cans to see which are empty.

"No. I'm ..."

The sound of several cars skidding around the track drowns me out, as mud sprays at us through the chain-link fence.

The man nods, as if he'd heard.

"Buckshot looking good in his laps," he says. "Run a couple of good ones."

"Who's Buckshot?"

He spits. "Buckshot going to be tough. Balzano looks good too. Don't know about old Boggs."

There are, at the dirt stock races on a Saturday night, all sorts of spectators. Groups of old men who sit on lawn chairs and chew tobacco, spitting it out in the grass. Groups of old women who do crosswords and knit and occasionally look at the racetrack. Families who have spread blankets and brought sandwiches and sodas as if they're on a picnic. Couples who spend most of the evening back by the souvenir stands, where they can hear one another talk, and neck, but can't see the track. Children who are buoyed by the fantasy of driving one day—or the opportunity to later meet the racers, Buckshot, Balzano. Some of these people are racing fans. They have stopwatches and scribble times on their programs. But most are just here because everyone else is, because there's nothing more exciting to do in eastern Ohio on a Saturday night than be at the stock car races. They're like the teenagers of Romney, West Virginia, who gather every Saturday night in the parking lots and drive up and down the main street, looking at one another.

"Buckshot," a man on the other side of me says, "is running real good." The man, who is bearded and also missing several teeth, puts some chewing tobacco in his mouth.

"Who's Buckshot?"

"Bob Adams, Jr., the local favorite."

The man who sold me the beer cuts timber during the week and sometimes comes out on Friday or Saturday and races in the street car category. There's nothing, he says, like the sensation of being in a race car under the lights on a Saturday night. His name is Rudy.

"You ever been in a race car?"

"Nope."

"Well, you're missing out on just a little bit of the power of life, then."

Rudy is a born-again Christian, although on one arm he has a tattoo of a serpent wrapping itself around the torso of a naked woman. "People are strange creatures," he tells me, leaning over and talking to my ear as the practice laps continue. "Biggest mistake we make is passing judgment. That's how I define religion: reserving judgment. When you get in a race car, and you're taking a turn at ninety miles an hour, you don't have time for thoughts like that, you don't have time to pass judgment or think what I consider to be sinful thoughts. You can't afford to. It's about as close as you can get to a religious experience."

The men in front of us are smoking corncob pipes now. Two old women are drinking Pabst Blue Ribbons right up by the fence and laughing at something.

"You know what they say this is?" Rudy asks, handing me his binoculars and pointing at something in the pit area. "The only truly American sport. Every other sport was derived from somewhere else. This is the only one that's truly American."

To really appreciate dirt stock racing, you need to go down into the pit area, Rudy explains, and I soon learn why. In the pits, the mood is more urgent. The sound of engines is maddening. The drivers shout at greasy-handed mechanics in jumpsuits among the jumble of tools and tires.

"I want you to really feel the power of this sport," Rudy says, as he leads me briskly along the pit row where the warm air tastes of gasoline and exhaust. Okay, I nod. By being a passive adventurer, I allow myself to be led places by people. I reserve judgment.

"You want to drive?" he asks.

"What? Drive?"

Rudy introduces me to Darrell Willey, the owner of the track, and we speak without hearing a word the other says. Pit row is not the place for casual conversation. We stand there watching the mechanics adjust the engines. Rudy shouts into my ear: "The men and women driving tonight are part of a circuit called the STAR series, which races all summer in the Ohio Valley, western West Virginia and down into Kentucky. Eventually you get to know the drivers," he says.

When the street stocks come up, a friend of Rudy asks if I'm ready.

"Ready? No."

"Just one lap," Rudy says.

"I don't know."

"I want you to experience the power of racing."

"One lap?"

"One lap."

Okay. I pull on a racing suit and helmet and listen intently to the shouted instructions as they strap me into a dark blue Chevy.

"Now, ready? Just gun the engine. You're up."

I do. The car goes. First down a narrow lane through the crowded pit area, and then suddenly I'm in the open, on the oval, being watched by hundreds of spectators. Circling the track, driving full speed into the glare of the grandstand lights is, as he had stated, a thrill. I push eighty on the straightaway, slide on mud going around the turn, then floor the car again on the back straightaway.

When I reach the pit area, the car now splattered with mud, I want to go around again, but they're signaling me in.

Rudy knows. He knows just what I feel. He can't stop grinning.

They're selling Pabst Blue Ribbons now for two dollars at the grandstand.

"You're buzzed," Rudy says several times, referring not to the beer but to the lap. He's enjoying it as much as I am. The intoxication of driving lingers, the feel of the engine.

"It's a sensation," he says, "of self-realization. Knowing how powerful you are. When you're out behind the wheel, you're at the center of things. You can't slip away, you have to be alert, you have to be alive. It puts you at the center of life."

I grin politely. People walk back and forth, wearing "Buckshot" Bob Adams T-shirts. Rudy tells me how Willey established the "No Beer" section several years ago out of respect for the religious people in this area. "There's a lot of religious people around, and there was a few complaints, so it was felt it should be done. A lot of racers themselves won't go on Sundays. That's just the nature of the area."

Coming up at intermission, says the evening's announcer, is "Mike Rossi and the Doomsday Chair"—an act in which a man will sit on a wooden chair packed full of dynamite and blow himself up.

"How does it work?" I ask one of the fellows next to me.

"You got me. There's plenty of crazy motherfuckers in this world."

"It's a gimmick," says Rudy, who is chewing tobacco. "I've seen it. He blows himself up every night in the summer. Never much worse for the wear."

The talk in the stands is suddenly late model, and I feel as if I'm missing out. I ask Rudy at one point how he'd define late model. In layman's terms.

"It's a full-fledged race car, with a tubular chassis, coiled-over spring ..."

I can't hear the rest.

Out on the track, Judy White, number sixty-five, is taking her laps. She's from Charleston, Rudy shouts, "owner of one of the largest landfills in the East."

"That's Larry Bond," he says, pointing. "He's late model. He cuts timber too. Now, there's big Porky Shores, you'll see him get out of his car and howl like a wolf at the end of the race."

As we wait for the races to start, Rudy's friend explains to me how the stocks have changed, his tobacco-scented breath against my ear: "It used to be stock cars meant one thing. But guys stretched the rules, see? Created what was a modified 'jig' car. No stock frame but just a tubular chassis and a thin sheet of metal. Okay? Then they put a flat nose on the car. In the late seventies, they brought out the 'wedge car,' where they added high plexiglass spoilers on the back, sticking straight up. So, track records kept dropping. And the motors went up, to fifty thousand dollars. Some track owners will pay an extra hundred dollars in prize money now if you've got a stock-appearing nose rather than a wedge nose."

The kind of car I drove, he says, was a street stock—"regular car, with a new engine and rear-end casing and fat tires."

I ask him how safe it is, racing street stocks, wondering if I could modify the old Ford, giving her a new rear-end casing and mag wheels.

"It's safe," he says. "The guys out there on the track are safer than the drivers who tow the cars to the tracks."

"It's a very safe sport," Rudy adds.

We sit through the practice laps and the qualifying heats, staring out at the track. By the time it comes to the semifinals, our clothes are plastered with mud. At the start of intermission, Mike Rossi walks out onto the track to scattered applause. His aides begin setting up the "Doomsday Chair," rigging the dynamite. An ambulance pulls up twenty feet from the chair and parks. The trick, the announcer says, will be this: Rossi sits on a wooden chair packed with one and a quarter sticks of dynamite. The dynamite blows and Rossi survives.

In a hushed tone, the announcer warns the audience: "If you have a hearing device, please turn it down *now*. If you are standing, please be seated *immediately*, or the force of this explosion will knock you down. Please, we don't want anyone to get hurt or killed."

Rossi, the announcer goes on, has done this trick now 167 times. But before settling down to be blown up again, Rossi takes the microphone and explains dramatically how he has a bad feeling about tonight.

"Each time it becomes more dangerous than the time before," he says. "I don't know why, but I'm more scared tonight than I've ever been in the years I've been doing this."

The audience is quiet, although there is some scoffing behind us. "Where's he going to go?" someone asks.

"He ain't going nowhere. He's sitting on it."

"Shit."

A woman says, "I thought they were shooting him out of a cannon."

"Shee-it."

An old man taps me on the shoulder, says, "That's what we're paying our extry two dollars for tonight."

He winks.

Finally, as much of the crowd covers its ears, the chair explodes. Pieces of wood shower down over the track, and through the smoke we see Rossi, lying on the dirt, completely still.

"I think he's dead," says the man next to me.

"Just wait," says another man.

The ambulance crew sprints to his assistance. The cherry top of the ambulance goes on. The audience is standing as paramedics work on him; at last, with apparent difficulty, Mike Rossi stands up. He limps, waves at the crowd. The applause is deafening.

It's a clear, pleasant evening now, with a full Ohio moon. The track announcer, Don Everhart, asks the crowd to take off their caps for the singing of the national anthem. Nearly everyone is wearing a cap.

The main event is twenty cars going forty laps in the invigorating Ohio night. The winner of the late model race gets two thousand dollars, and the six leaders in the series are all here tonight for this memorial event. "There's nothing in the world like the cars going around the first turn." Rudy grins. "If you thought it was a kick doing a practice lap, you should try this."

Indeed, none of the preliminary events prepares one for the speed and competitiveness of this race. The crowd remains standing for the first few laps and even after they sit, there's no talking. Everyone stares, raptly, out at the track. Rudy yells at me frequently, but it's impossible to tell what he's saying. Each time I nod.

Jack Boggs is the leader for most of the race, and after he gets the checkered flag, he stops his car and steps out on the edge of the track to wave. There's loud booing from the beer section. The regular section, though, cheers modestly.

"Why are they booing?" I ask Rudy. He's booing too.

"Why are they booing him?" I ask after it stops.

He shrugs. "No reason."

As soon as the first few cars cross the finish, the people begin filing out.

"Aw, he's a hot dog," Rudy laughs.

"Who, Boggs?"

"Yeah."

"He's not from around here?"

"Hell, no, that's what they's booing him for. He beat Bob Adams. Boggs is from Kentucky."

The power of the race stays with me afterward. Driving the winding roads in the moonlight in the old Ford, my clothes a mud suit, I feel the clutch of new adventures in the dips of the roadway. The racers, the spectators, they're all set now, energized, as if what they're driving back to is something other than their weekday lives.

For the rest of the evening, and for several days afterward, I think of ways to get back out on the track. To go around again, just a couple more laps under those grandstand lights.

Main Town

I n southern Ohio, tall stalks of corn turn slowly brown on thirsty late summer afternoons. Farm towns dot the highway. Women hang laundry on long lines beside wood-frame houses, and giant tractors frequently block the two-lane road. In each of these hamlets I stop, sometimes for a day or two, and explore and listen.

In Bourneville (named for Ohio mapmaker Alexander Bourne), a farmer, whose overalls seem several sizes too big, tells me with possessive certainty about the early days of the turnpike.

"Timbered Ohio was the first land anyone thought of as 'The West,'" he says. "You wanted to get to the wide open Far West, you had to cut a path through these woods 'cause the timberland don't stop 'til you get to Kansas.

"This was a mail route here before it became a turnpike. Eventually, they opened it up as the old Cinsennati Turnpike. Back in the mid-1800s. Went all the way to Cinsennati. Had toll gates all along. Even had one here in Bourneville. At each toll gate, there was a long pole that swung on a pivot. You know what a pivot is? The pole they called a pike. When the fare was paid, they turned the pike and let you pass. That's where the name come from—turnpike.

"Now the term 'gate-crasher'—some Chillicothe youngbloods can take credit for that. They got it in mind that they was going to break through the toll gate without paying, and so they got to calling them gate-crashers. That's a true story."

In Albany, at the Hocking River Trading Post, a man shows me some bluegill and largemouth bass he has just caught, and then says he bets I'm headed to Chillicothe.

"How do you know?"

"Oh, I can tell."

He chuckles, and the other men in the trading post do too. The talk turns to the corn crop but eventually comes back to Chillicothe.

"People in Chillicothe," he says, "just tend to be a little bit big-headed, I guess you could say. Always have been."

"Big-headed?" I ask. "In what way?"

"I don't know. They just tend to think they're a little bit better than other folks."

"Well, I don't think that."

"No, sir. I didn't say you did."

"But you said you could tell I was heading to Chillicothe?"

He stands in the doorway and looks outside at Highway 50. There is no response.

Chillicothe is a Shawnee Indian word meaning "main town." Once it was in the heart of Shawnee territory—Tecumseh's land—before settlers pushed west from Virginia and Kentucky and took over. Nowadays, it's probably best known for its leviathan paper industry, although in the summer the town remembers the Shawnee with a celebration called Feast of the Flowering Moon.

"This was the land of Tecumseh," I am told in a Chillicothe pancake house by historian John Barber, who claims to be part Navajo. "I have a family tree to prove it," he says, in case I don't believe him. We're sitting at the counter, eating pancakes. "These days, everybody claims to be part Native American. The Native American population has tripled in two years, supposedly, but most of them can't prove they really are. Tecumseh tried to save this land. He tried to confederate the Indian nation to fight against the white man."

"But he failed?"

"He failed. Because there *was* no Indian nation. It was a land of Indian nations. It wasn't just one. *Shawnee* means 'People from the South.' They came to central Ohio from down in the Mississippi Valley in the 1600s."

"How about Tecumseh?"

"Tecumseh came along in the 1700s. He was a documented clairvoyant. He predicted the 1811 earthquake. He was not a benign figure, though. He was truly a noble savage. Tecumseh hated the white man with a vengeance. His brother was called The Prophet. He had visionary powers also."

He pours more syrup onto his plate and wipes a triangle of pancake over it. The traffic light changes, and the gray Ohio sky fills with black diesel smoke from the heavy trucks rumbling by. Barber sips his coffee. His expression is solemn.

"Well, if they had all these powers," I say, "why couldn't they keep the white man out?"

"Because the white man had a different kind of power. Mentally, they were equipped with different weapons. It was never a fair fight."

In 1812, the year before Tecumseh was killed in battle, the Chillicothe paper industry was born beside Kinnikinnick Creek. The first railroad line came through forty years later, opening up the city for trade; by 1890, there were more than eleven thousand people living in Chillicothe. In 1892, Colonel Daniel Mead bought the city's paper mill and established Mead Paper.

I spend days wandering this Indian land, near Chillicothe, nicknamed the Valley of the Kings. In the neat green hills, there are as many as five thousand Hopewell and Adena Indian burial mounds—more, some say, than anywhere else in the country. It is a colorful, mystical world in late summer, with flocks of wildflowers on many of the hillsides and long stretches of pastureland that shimmer in the sun. But it is the long-ago presence of the Indians that really gives the land life. I travel to the mounds: Seip, Mound City and, the most impressive, Serpent, which winds along the east bluff of Ohio Creek. Serpent Mound is a twisting image in the hot Ohio landscape, and one with contrary meanings: Good. Evil. Eternity. Repentance. Shedding skin. I think of Rudy at the stock car races in Stewart, with his tattoo of a serpent wrapped around a naked woman.

At Fort Hill, I hike up into an isolated land that hasn't changed much in a thousand years. Among the oaks along the northeast slope there is a sound of creek water and a smell of bark. In the sunlight are Canada violets and buttercups. A wave of surprisingly cool air pulls through the trees as I near the top.

The Land Butchers

S hortly after I meet Lester and Jean Wallis on the main road through Hillsboro, Ohio, Jean backs her car, full speed, into the front of the old Ford.

"Whoops."

"You weren't paying attention that time," her husband says.

"I forgot he was parked there."

The three of us get out of her car, slowly, to have a look. But the damage to the old Ford is minor.

I shrug.

"You have to pay a little closer attention," Lester says, and the three of us get back into her little car, Jean and I up front, Lester in the back.

Lester Wallis is a tall, stooped man, who walks with a limp and talks slowly—the antithesis of his wife, who is short and filled with nervous energy. The Wallises run the Highland House Museum in Hillsboro. When I expressed interest in the town's history and in the local Indian lore, Jean Wallis insisted I take a drive with them to see some of the county's notable sights.

As we head out into the country, Lester recollects what it was like growing up in Hillsboro, back when the farms all had fences and people traded goods instead of buying them.

"We traded chickens and eggs for most of what we needed," he says. "It was a good system. People traded us things we didn't have, and we traded them things they didn't have. Efficient way to live. Wouldn't hurt if people went back to that old way. One time, Dad added a room on to a fellow's house, and he was paid with a cow and a thirty-eight-caliber pistol."

The car tops a rise too fast; it feels like we're going to take off.

"You're driving seventy now, Jean."

"Oh, Lester."

"Yes, you are."

The air is cool. The car windows become fogged. Jean turns on both the heater and the defroster. It's soon unbearably warm, and I roll down a window.

"You're driving too fast," Lester says.

"Well, no, I'm not."

She slams on her brakes as a leaf blows across the road, then tailgates at thirty miles per hour for several miles until the car in front turns off.

Jean's voice sounds like a tour guide's: "The Seven Caves are back over there, an intricate network of caverns and old Indian trails. Daniel Boone camped there in 1778. He was captured by Indians and tied to a beech tree. They've got a tree down there now that they've named 'Boone's Tree,' but if you look closely at it, it isn't even a real beech. They take a little liberty telling that story. Now Rocky Fork Creek is back this way," she says, looking off to the right.

"Watch the road."

"Lester."

"It was the Northwest Ordinance that really changed things," Lester says, taking over the narrative so that Jean will concentrate on the driving. "Brought immigrants out here and said they could have their own farms. That was one of the last things that pushed the Indian out."

Suddenly, Jean Wallis slams on her brakes, and the car stops.

"Fox squirrel," she says.

A red squirrel with a bushy tail runs across the road in front of us and off behind some trees. Behind us, a car stops, then goes around, the driver shaking his head.

Lester leans forward, as we start up again, to give me a rundown on squirrels. "You may be unfamiliar with the fox squirrel. But that's the big squirrel here in Hillsboro. Now, of course, the gray squirrel, which you probably know, well, there isn't much to the gray squirrel. It's too small. Nobody likes the gray squirrel. But the fox squirrel is just about the size—oh, about the size of a regular rabbit. Now, we don't have jackrabbits around here, just the regular cottontails. And the fox squirrel is the main squirrel around here. Just about the size of a cottontail."

"Lester, stop, he's not interested in squirrels."

Lester doesn't talk for a while after that.

They show me some other places: a one-room schoolhouse, an old mill and the remains of an Indian fort. Then Jean drives into the Appalachian foothills, hills that all have names, mostly of the pioneer families who originally settled on them. She points them out as we pass: Butler Hill, Reed Hill, Graham Hill. ... All have massive clearings now and the pungent smell of cut timber.

"See what they've been doing?" Jean asks. "That makes me sick."

"What's going to happen is that the topsoil's going to slide down to the bottom and form a clay crown," Lester says. "They're what I call land butchers. Anytime they tear something down that shouldn't be torn down, they call it progress."

"Look at all the timber they're cutting," Jean says, stopping in the middle of the road. "And the man who owns that land won the lottery too."

"People get a little money, they only want more," Lester says, still leaning forward, looking at the speedometer as Jean picks up speed again. "You can't satisfy the wanting for money."

"He won four hundred thousand dollars."

"They're never satisfied."

We come into Sinking Springs, the first settlement in the county, dating to 1795. Jean Wallis insists that I see the old schoolhouse, a building the Wallises have helped to restore. During the Civil War, it was used as a guardhouse.

"Let me show you," she says.

"No, I wouldn't drive out there," Lester says curtly.

"It's all gravel underneath, Lester."

"But it's soaked."

"Lester."

She drives out onto the grass behind the building. Soon the back wheels are spinning, and we're no longer moving.

"Reverse it."

"Lester, I can't. I can't go forward or backward."

Lester and I get out, and for ten minutes we push on the back of the car as Jean guns the engine and the tires spin. Mud shoots all over us; I feel like I'm at the stock car races again. Back and forth we rock it, as the tires turn and the engine roars. Finally, the car moves, and I look at Lester, who resembles a creature in a bad horror movie.

"There we go," he says.

"Well." Jean Wallis looks at me sheepishly as we start off again. "That was an experience."

All the way back to Hillsboro, Lester and I pull mud from our clothes and throw it out the windows.

"You're going to have to be more careful," Lester says at one point. Jean does not respond.

In a little town called Carmel, she stops at an intersection and waits.

"You don't have a stoplight there," Lester says.

"I know that. I'm waiting for this man, Lester."

The man, though, is just standing on the curb looking at us. Jean Wallis waves him across the street. The man waves back.

As the sun goes down on the old Ohio street, Highway 50 again, the Wallises treat me to dinner at Bob's Big Boy to make up for the mud. I feel good sitting there with them, being introduced to practically everyone who passes by the table, all of whom kid us about the mud that has dried in our hair and on our necks.

When I'm alone in my room that night, the air is crisp through the screen, and I lie awake for several hours. A colder season looms.

More than a century ago, one of the most noted temperance episodes took place in Hillsboro. Some natives still claim it was what eventually led to the great national Prohibition of the 1920s. A few days before Christmas, a Boston preacher named Dio Lewis came to Hillsboro to give a fiery lecture about the evils of alcohol. The women of Hillsboro were so inspired by his talk that they launched a crusade to close the town's thirteen saloons and liquor dispensaries. Seventy women participated. They entered the saloons and sang hymns. They prayed. One by one, the saloons closed down.

Nowadays, Hillsboro is a good drinking town again, and before leaving, I stop in the town's most notorious saloon, the North High Lounge, for a beer. Several years ago, country music singer Johnny Paycheck shot a man here during an argument.

It's a small, dingy place, and the customers are all men. They're amiable, and all have tales to tell about Donny Lytle, which is Paycheck's real name.

"He's a good guy, but he tended to get into a little trouble when he drank," says a big pot-bellied man wearing a leather jacket. "That song of his says a lot about him. That's how he felt about things."

"'Take This Job and Shove It,'" another man fills in.

The guy he shot was a wise guy, they tell me. And his name also happened to be Wise. He was a taxidermist. All of the men claim to have been in here the night it happened, some earlier in the evening, some right when the shot was fired. But their stories differ.

"He was drinking and started in on what was at first a friendly argument with some men. There was a hunter and a taxidermist. Paycheck shot the taxidermist."

"Why the taxidermist?"

"He took his pick."

"What were they arguing about?"

"The story is, turtle meat."

"I'd say there was more to it than that, though," says a tall, severe man with scars on his cheeks and across his nose.

"See, Donny grew up kind of poor," says the big man. "He didn't have a whole lot. There's a story that when he was little, his family couldn't afford much, so they had to eat turtle meat."

"Nah," the tall man says, "there's more to it than that."

"He quit school in the seventh grade and made a name for himself. I think he didn't handle success so well."

"I wouldn't say that. He was ornery. He was always getting into trouble. Little stuff. He'd always been like that."

"Well, he's a little guy, too," says the big man. "He's only five foot five."

"People liked him, though. A lot of people looked up to him for what he'd done."

"Did he live here?" I ask.

"He was living in Georgia at the time. But he used to come up to visit his mother a lot. She lives in Greenfield, still."

"So what about the night of the shooting?" I ask. "What happened?"

"Well, like I say, there was a bit of drinking. And these guys were standing back over there, I think."

"Over there," the other man says.

"And they offered Donny a place to stay and a dinner featuring turtle meat. And a few words were exchanged and Donny pulled out his gun."

"What he said was his security people suggested he wear it."

"Yeah, and he still says the gun went off accidentally."

"The bullet hit Wise in the head. It didn't kill him, but Paycheck spent several years in jail for the shooting."

We drink beer, and the story of Johnny Paycheck is embellished some more. As I walk back to the motel, I am shivering. I respond to the cold with motion. It is time to leave Hillsboro.

Frank

I begin to discover, after several months on the road, that there is no shortage of people who have undertaken journeys similar to mine, who have somewhere left behind a stable life for an undefined search. Out on the road, you begin to notice the other people who are not anchored to anything, and they notice you. As I count how much money is left in the tackle box, I realize that perhaps this is the only thing—what's left in the tackle box— keeping me from being like some of those people.

On the road outside of Hillsboro, an old man is hitchhiking, and I stop to pick him up. His clothes, I see as he gets in, are mismatched and tattered, and give off a stench. His name is Frank, he tells me. He pulls out a crumpled pack of Camels and lights one.

"Where to?" I ask him.

"Cincinnati. Looking for work. How far you going?"

"Cincinnati. What type of work?"

"Anything they got to offer."

The soles of his shoes, I see, are worn down and ripped; he is only wearing one sock. He sucks deeply on the cigarette and doesn't seem to let all the smoke out.

"I've been to New York, Memphis, Richmond, Parkersburg. Can't find nothing," he says.

It is difficult to understand him, I think because he has only a few teeth left. His troubles suddenly interest me.

"How long have you been out of work?"

"Seven years."

"Seven *years*?"

"Well, you fall off, you never get back on. Each pass, you find it a little harder. But it ain't been for lack of trying."

He laughs, and it turns into a long, agonizing coughing spell.

"Where are you from?" I ask.

He thinks about it. "I guess Cleveland, as much as anyplace. Richmond. I spent many years in Richmond."

"What did you do?"

"Done everything. Whatever you got. Years ago, lived down in Richmond and worked for the telephone company. For fourteen years. Oh, I found out they was doing some things."

"Things?"

"Yep. I found out all about it, which is maybe where I went wrong. I tried Phoenix and I tried Memphis and I tried New York. Nothing."

Late in the afternoon, we come to the mishmash of Cincinnati, a river city near the Indiana border, where the last of the day's sun is mirrored orange in the windows of office buildings. Light drains from the sky; internal lights suddenly start reflecting onto the long, green lawns. Cincinnati, like most old towns, was created in response to the country's early transportation system. It was an important stop on the Ohio River. But Highway 50 passes by, not through, Cincinnati, as it does nearly all of the large cities along the way. The paths it traces are older.

The highway runs for a while beside the Ohio, through a run-down stretch of abandoned buildings, motorcycle shops, refineries, grain towers, mountains of salt and tanks of petroleum. Barges are being loaded. The air smells of chemicals. Up the road is North Bend, the fourth settlement in Ohio (1789) and the birthplace of William Henry Harrison, ninth president of the United States, who died of pneumonia a month after the inauguration. Frank and I walk up the hillside in this old town full of junk cars and read the inscription on the huge monument commemorating Harrison.

After crossing into Indiana, another state named after Indians, I stop for groceries: fruit, cheese, tomatoes, lettuce, mustard, bread, sodas. We eat thick sandwiches on a bench down by the rushing Ohio. Frank chews loudly and with great difficulty, like a dog with a piece of gristle, twisting his head, turning toward the sun for a while with a pained expression. He has changed his mind, he tells me, after successfully swallowing, about Cincinnati.

"I guess I might as well try for Kansas City, if I want to be serious. Ain't nothing in Cincinnati."

"How do you know?"

"Been going to Cincinnati all my life. Don't need to waste any more time there."

What this means, I realize, is that he wants to stay with me. He wants to hitch aboard this journey I'm on, which is fresher and less disillusioned than his. A respite from his own lonely travels.

"I'm not traveling straight through, though," I say, squinting at him in the bright morning light. "I think I'm going to stop for a while in Lawrenceburg or Aurora."

"Don't bother me."

He eats another piece of his sandwich, not talking for a long time. A faint, steady, pained noise emanates from his throat. After he swallows, he begins another coughing fit. When he finishes, he pulls out a Camel.

We're entering the bottomlands of southeastern Indiana, where the towns have names like Rising Sun and Aurora and Friendship. Each spring, the Ohio River floods this land, recharging the Great Miami aquifer system and leaving a rich cover for farmers. Most of the floods are mild, but someday there will be a big one, like the flood of 1937, which devastated Lawrenceburg. Everyone knows it and accepts it the way people in California accept earthquakes and people in Florida accept hurricanes.

As the sun reaches high into the clear Indiana sky, I park by another stretch of the Ohio and tell Frank I'm going on alone. He just looks at me. I shake hands with him, feeling the dirt crusted on his fingers. He won't say good-bye or even acknowledge that I'm leaving. He's still watching, I see, holding a piece of a cheese sandwich, as I get in the car again.

At a lounge in Lawrenceburg that evening, I meet a boorish casketmaker with a thick head of black hair. He works for Aurora Casket, he tells me, inventor of the stainless-steel coffin and the largest producer of caskets in the country.

"That's what this town is noted for, if you want to know the truth: Aurora Casket. Casket capital of the country. People don't think about where caskets come from, but this is it. Aurora, Indiana. You didn't know that, did you?"

"No."

"You know what our biggest trouble is? You can only interest so many people in a casket. Know what I'm saying? Your market is always restricted by the fact that only two million people die each year in the United States."

"I hadn't thought of that."

"Oh, yeah. It's different from other businesses. Take car makers. A lot more you can do marketing-wise with cars."

He smiles. His petite wife sits beside him at the bar, not speaking. She chain-smokes steadily, turning her head and exhaling the smoke from a tiny corner of her mouth. I think at first that she is annoyed with him for talking so loudly, but then I realize it is just her manner.

"On top of everything else, you've got cremation up to eighteen percent now, and that's hurting the business. This part of the country is unique. This is where the auto industry began. But the banks in Indiana weren't supportive, so it moved north. To Detroit. Now the major industries in Aurora are whiskey and caskets." The man's wife, very slowly, lets out a long, steady stream of smoke into the air. I leave after one drink.

In the morning, I see Frank standing by the fence in front of the motel, halfheartedly hitchhiking. He acts surprised to see me and waves as I come out of the room.

"Shit," he says, coughing, coming over, "I looked all over this goddamn town. Can't find nothing. I'm going to have to try Kansas City."

We both look up and down Highway 50.

"Goddamn Indiana. Never was good for much of nothing."

"Well, good luck," I say and shake his hand again. He watches me. Clearly I have hurt his feelings.

I set out west on Highway 50 but after several miles turn around, thinking that I will pick Frank up and take him to Kansas City. Back in Lawrenceburg and Aurora, there is no sign of him, though. I never see Frank again.

Larrison's

I n the Rexall pharmacy outside Lawrenceburg, I lose an hour. The clerk explains why. Indiana's way of telling time is the most confusing of any state in the country. Seventy-six Indiana counties use eastern standard time year-round; eleven use central standard time in winter and central daylight time in summer; five use eastern standard time in winter, but switch to eastern daylight time in summer. Lawrenceburg went to what Indiana people call "fast time" in April. But if you drive just a little to the west, all of the clocks are still on "slow time."

Some people refuse to change their time. "You'll find house-holds that keep two different times," the woman in the pharmacy tells me. "We just have to ask each other a lot, 'Is that fast time or slow time?' A lot of places, the kids'll go to school on slow time, but the parents work on fast time."

In slow time, Highway 50 crosses the till plains to the interior low plains, through Ripley County and Versailles State Park, into the uplands where the road is flanked by beech and oak and hickory and on to Seymour.

Late in the day, on the eastern edge of Seymour, the radio turns to static and the dashboard lights fade. I pull into the first garage I come to. A dirty mechanic ambles over.

"You got a fire?"

"Pardon?"

"Smells like you got a fire. Get out."

"I don't think so."

With trepidation, the stooped ectomorphic man raises the hood, waving me away.

"Stand back," he says.

"I think it's the alternator," I say. Irritated, he indicates I'm standing too close.

"You got insurance on this thing?"

"Sure."

He's wiping his hands on a rag, standing back like the engine could burst into flames at any minute.

"What do you think?"

"I think you're lucky," he says. "Planning on staying in Seymour a couple of days?"

"Not really."

"Well, you'd better ought to plan on it."

"What's wrong with it?"

"For starters?" He looks at me like I'm crazy. "You got gas leaking out, number one. You're missing your alternator belt, number two. And on top of that, you got several parts in here that don't even belong. You pulled in here just in time, friend. That's the good news. The bad news is, you're going to need half of this engine rebuilt before you can expect to go anywhere."

"I'll take an alternator belt," I say. "And check the leak."

The man says he can't get to it until morning, but he offers to give me a lift into town. He'll be ready in "just a minute," he says, and disappears into the washroom for nearly forty-five. I wait in the service station, paging through the telephone book and a pamphlet for Uniroyal tires. He comes out from the washroom at last, all clean and smelling of cheap soap and toothpaste. His hair is slicked back with water and his demeanor is suddenly upbeat. He has changed personalities along with his clothes.

"Ready?" he says, waving a gym bag. "That's my pickup right out there."

A middle-aged man who could pass for a cancer patient, he drives quickly, enjoying himself, passing, darting in and out of lanes, as if driving home were an amusement park ride. Occasionally, he turns his head into the wind and whistles "Strangers in the Night."

When I ask him what *Hoosier*, the state motto, means, he's taken aback. I immediately regret asking.

"Hoosier?"

"Yeah."

"Hoosier."

"Yeah."

To pass a Subaru, he guns the engine to seventy-five. His face is suddenly, for a few moments, flushed.

"That's just what they call it. The 'Hoosier State.' That's Indiana. Heck, I don't know, it's just a name."

Clearly, he is not satisfied with his explanation. Several times he comes back to the subject as he drives rapidly through the rush hour traffic, trying, it seems, to formulate a more suitable reply. "Actually, there was a story about Hoosier. Something about somebody knocking on a door and someone else answering and saying 'Who's 'er?' Hoosier. Something like that. It's just an offhand sort of thing, near as I can tell."

To change the subject, I ask him about business in Seymour, and he seems relieved to be able to talk with authority again.

"Well, see, the nature of the economy is such that the Midwest is getting immigrants these days. Used to be it was just the coasts. A lot of new industry has come to Seymour, though, and we're starting to get more and more immigrants because of it. The big thing now is we've got several Japanese firms, which is changing the flavor of Seymour. Some people don't like it. I don't mind, because it brings me more business. Want to stop at Larrison's?"

He parks the pickup by a corner restaurant downtown, and we go in for a cup of coffee. The gray, shimmering twilight air feels pleasantly cool. Men are lined up here at the counter, drinking coffee and eating pie—their day's reward.

Larrison's, a red-brick restaurant with a green, red and white awning, serves a special function in Seymour. It seems to bridge the distance between what this town was—a small agricultural community where everybody knew everybody else—and what it is becoming— a thriving industrial town, full of fast-food franchises and foreign investors. Everyone, it seems, comes into Larrison's: town officials, business owners, farmers, the Japanese and the retired old-timers. It is a safe, unchanging haven in the center of a changing community.

During the several days I am in Seymour, I go to Larrison's for breakfast and again in the afternoons and talk with owner Ed Larrison, who remembers the days before fast food, when he'd keep his little restaurant open until eight every night. Fast food made him change it to seven, then six. Now he closes up at five, when the business day ends.

Ed Larrison, owner of Larrison's, a favorite hangout in Seymour, Indiana.

"Back then, the franchises stayed away from the small towns like this one," he says. "But they don't care anymore. They'll go anywhere. I've seen twenty, twenty-five restaurants open up since I've been here. Eventually they're going to force this one out of business, I suppose. They've already taken away the dinner business. But every time I go to a fast-food restaurant, you know what I see? A line. Seems like it's sort of defeating the purpose."

Larrison comes from Columbus, Ohio, and his wife from North Vernon. Seymour, originally, was to them a neutral territory. "We looked at the map and picked a spot that wasn't too close to any of our in-laws. Seymour seemed just about right."

One of Larrison's business philosophies is to encourage a varied clientele. "I welcome all sorts," he says. "We've had them all: rich, poor, homeless. We had one guy, he used to sleep in the alleys. We called him Lightning. He was always dressed in dirty clothes, and he'd take out a rag and wipe the table and we'd have to disinfect. I never told him he couldn't come in; I never did that with anybody. But sometimes he'd just smell so bad. I hated to do it, but sometimes I'd have to tell him, 'It's time to go jump in the river again.' One time I guess it hit him the wrong way and he's never come back." I think about Frank as he says this and wonder if it could be the same person.

One day I'm sitting at the counter in Larrison's when Sonny Mellencamp, John Cougar Mellencamp's father, walks by.

Rock star Mellencamp grew up here in Seymour and, in recent years, has become something of a troubadour for the small town. He sings about the plight of midwesterners: farmers and people who live and die in small towns. One of his songs, "Pink Houses," plays on the jukebox, with the chorus, "Ain't that America." When you enter Seymour, there's a sign on Highway 50: "Birthplace of John Cougar Mellencamp."

"What is it that gives people such pride in Seymour?" I ask Sonny Mellencamp.

"Living here."

"But there seems to be something else here, a unique spirit."

"Can't say. This is where I live."

Sonny Mellencamp is cordial but private. Being interviewed does not interest him.

"There's plenty of other people who can tell you about Seymour," he says.

At Larrison's, the talk sometimes turns to Mellencamp's son. Ed Larrison remembers John Mellencamp as typical of the kids in Seymour, only more determined. "I think that's probably what set him apart. He worked so darn hard at it. I'll have to admit, I can't understand all the lyrics. But he wanted to succeed and he did."

Geri Schepman, who works at the Chamber of Commerce, says it still amazes her what happened to him. "It blows my mind," she says. "I just didn't see it. I knew he was very strong-willed and determined, but I just didn't see him becoming famous. He was okay, but I've heard people sing that are a whole lot better. I didn't pay attention to his songs, I guess. His brother Joe could sing a lot better than him back then."

An older woman, sitting at the counter, says that when he first became a star, John Mellencamp did not appreciate Seymour enough. "That bothered some of us. He seemed like he'd forgotten where he came from. But eventually, he realized that this was home. He's given Seymour a good name now. But the town's helped him too. It's a mutual thing."

When the old Ford is finally ready, the mechanic warns me that it really isn't. "Your alternator belt's fine now. But the way that engine is cooking, you'll have a fire on your hands before you hit the Illinois line. I suggest you have that whole thing gone over part by part. I can get to it tomorrow, early if you like."

"You say there'll be a fire by the Illinois line."

"I guarantee it."

"Literally?"

He smiles.

"Well, if this service station allowed for such things, yes. But seeing as it doesn't, I can't, literally, give you a guarantee. But, figuratively, I will."

I write down his name and address in my notebook and decide to send him a postcard from somewhere out west, if, that is, the old Ford doesn't burn up between here and Illinois.

Before leaving Seymour, I stop one last time at Larrison's for a slice of pie and a glass of milk.

Lime Temples

T he edges of the continent do not sufficiently tell the tale of how all this land became a country. What they offer is an abbreviated, romanticized version. It is the middle country, the mysterious region of rivers and immense open spaces, that contains the real story.

The East's monuments to progress and proficiency owe much to little midwestern towns such as Bedford, Indiana—including, in this case, the stone that they were made of. The Empire State Building, the National Cathedral, the Pentagon and the Metropolitan Museum of Art were all constructed from sheets of limestone taken out of the earth around Bedford. The state's rolling limestone belt extends from Putnam County, in the north, down to Crawford County, but the heart of it is here, in the forested country that Highway 50 cuts through near Bedford.

A little ways past the Stone City Mall—on the same road as the Stone City Motel and the Stone City Restaurant—I stop at a gas station and ask what's so special about Indiana limestone.

"Just a question of quality," the attendant says. "You can always tell the difference between a building that's made of Indiana limestone and a building that's made of"—he looks at my license tag—"Maryland limestone, for instance."

"Does Maryland have limestone?"

"Every state has limestone. But no other state has Indiana limestone. Highest quality stone in the world."

"Why?"

"That's a question I guess only God can answer."

Lonesome in this somber stone city, where every house seems to have a birdbath and a stone bench, I remember that I know someone from the Bedford area—or did know someone, anyway—from college days. I decide to try giving her a call and am pleased to find that she is still living here, and remembers me.

"You were always reading the newspaper," she says. "You'd bring it to class and read it surreptitiously when the lectures got boring."

"It's funny what people remember."

"So did you become a journalist?"

"It so happens."

Kate is smaller than I remember, a waifish woman with a short punk-style haircut. "I grew up with this," she says when we meet at one of the quarries. "All kinds of stuff goes on out here. They've found stolen cars at the bottom of the quarries. People have gotten killed swimming in here. They hit their head on a rock and just drowned."

"Are you married?"

"Are you?"

"No."

"Divorced. Why are you here?"

"Traveling."

"Where?"

"Across the country. A slow, long journey to another life."

"Ah." The woman whose expertise, it seems, had once been poetry, squints at the bright quarry water. "Limestone, you know, is still the best job here," she says. "Always has been. My dad worked in the mill, and so did his dad. That's what you do if you live in Bedford."

The limestone industry, I learn, boomed here after the railroad came through in 1854 and stayed strong up until the 1930s. When the Depression arrived, builders sought cheaper construction materials, and the stone business dwindled. During the sixties and seventies, the limestone industry suffered again because of the proliferation of steel-and-glass structures. In the eighties, though, steel-and-glass buildings began showing cracks as they were pummeled by hurricanes, so there has been a resurgence in the limestone industry. People again want things that they know will last.

Kate, whose normal gait resembles that of a race walker, takes me on a tour. In the mills on the edge of town, giant slabs of limestone are cut to order with diamond-tipped gang saws. The saws, similar to chain saws, can move through the rock at a rate of ten feet per hour. Some of the blocks are then carved by hand to fit specific needs. In nearby quarries, the stone is broken apart by machines called channelers that resemble gigantic ice picks and lifted in twenty-ton blocks by gantry cranes.

By a creek in the nearby woods Kate leads me to a grave, all by itself, surrounded by a broken stone wall. Buried here is Winthrop Foote, one of the first men who understood the potential of the Indiana limestone industry. Foote came to the area in 1825 and founded Bluestone Quarry. At the time, bluestone was the most desired stone. It turns a blue shade when it's wet.

"What do you do now?" I ask her, as we stand by the grave. "You were a poet, back in college days."

She laughs.

"I've done a little of this and a little of that. I worked in California for three years, that's where I met my husband. He was transferred overseas. We lived in Kenya and Ghana and Somalia. We traveled in Europe for six months. Visited Japan."

"Did you stop writing?"

"Oh, not really," she says, without conviction. "But there are more practical concerns."

"So you're back in Bedford?"

"For now. I'm staying with my parents until I can find work."

We walk back up the path to the highway. Her stride is determined, as if she were intent on getting somewhere.

Before leaving Bedford, I meet Maxine Kruse, a former town official, who tells me the sad tale of the Bedford Pyramid. Back in the 1970s, a group of Egyptian businessmen came to Bedford with the idea of building a pyramid in the heart of the country's limestone belt. The pyramid was to have been modeled after the Great Pyramid built at Giza, Egypt, three thousand years ago. It would have been ninety-six feet high, one hundred and fifty-one feet at the base. Surrounding it was to be a limestone theme park.

Maxine drives a shiny red convertible with "Max" on the license plate. She was with the tourism department in the seventies, but says she quit over the pyramid deal. "There were some big plans. It could have gone. The pyramids in Egypt were made of limestone. And the Egyptians came here figuring if tourists saw a pyramid in Indiana, they'd want to go over to Egypt. They wanted us to do the feasibility study for it, and they'd fund all the rest. But we could never get the funding we needed to get the study done. The community thought it was too expensive and too frivolous. Senator William Proxmire gave Bedford his Golden Fleece Award for considering it."

On a muggy afternoon, Maxine drives me out to the site of what would have been the limestone theme park, explaining as we go some of the stone structures in town: the old jail, the churches with the twenty-four-inch-thick walls, the stone porches made by mill workers from stone scraps. The theme park land is now covered with weeds and broken stone, much of it painted over with obscene graffiti. Rusted trucks have "Limestone Tourist Park" painted on the side. The road into the park is cracked.

"I was disgusted with losing that pyramid deal," Maxine says, as we take a walkway down to the Empire Quarry. "Proxmire didn't know what he was talking about. The pyramid would have cost us just a drop in the bucket."

The air is full of insects and humidity, along this dirt path to the quarry ledge. Empire Quarry is a stunning sight, with its perfect cuts in the earth and clear green water.

"This could have been a great attraction. I think there's a new interest in tourism here. But I don't think you'll ever see the pyramid. The time for that passed.

"There's one compensation," she says as she drives around the corner and stops in front of a modest stone house. "One man wanted to make sure there was a pyramid in the area, so, as you can see, he built his own."

Indeed, on the front lawn is a small stone pyramid.

"His name is Diehl, and they call it the Diehl Pickle Pyramid. It cost him two thousand dollars. I guess it's better than nothing."

She lets me off back in town, and I thank her, surprised again at how accommodating strangers can be, how willing they are to play host for their towns, their worlds.

The Little Egypt Pancake House

T here are fires burning in the fields of Lawrence County and a cool smell of gasoline on the night wind as the old Ford and I enter Illinois, yet another state named for Indians. To someone unfamiliar with eastern Illinois, these fires in the night—which serve to burn gas off the oil that is pumped here—are startling. There are no signs explaining them.

There's nothing else to look at until I come to the Lawrence County Fair, where a sign announces tonight's main event: the tractor pull. I stop and park the Ford in a field.

The men here, and many of the women, are attired in caps that advertise farm and feed stores. Mine, which features the Washington Redskins insignia, seems out of place. Several times it gets confused stares as I stand, sipping a coke, by the grandstand.

A heavyset man with a surprisingly small head comes over and asks, aggressively it seems, "You pulling?"

"Not tonight," I say. "Didn't even bring the truck."

He looks askance at my Redskins cap and places his hands on his wide hips.

"It looks just a little slick tonight."

"Maybe."

"I'm pulling, in a six-thousand-pound, four-gear. What class do you pull?"

"Same."

"Manual?"

His face is flat. His stomach breathes steadily up and down. This is, I see, some sort of challenge.

I guess. "Automatic."

"No such class. If you go manual, how far you pull it?"

I shrug. "Get it all the way across the field sometimes."

"What's your best?"

"That's it."

"How many feet?"

"Don't remember."

"You pull two-fifty?"

"A few times."

He looks me up and down.

"I was ready for three hundred tonight, but it seems a little slick. Too bad, too. I've got her running real smooth. You from around here?"

"No. I'm not."

"Where you from?"

"Nearby," I say.

"Salem?"

"Yeah."

Now he gives me a long, and pointed, stare. What kind of a liar are you, anyway? it seems to ask.

Before the national anthem plays, the fair announcer asks us to stand and remove our caps. "With all the disrespect that's been given to it in recent days," he says, "we'd like to open with a proper singing of the anthem." He's referring, apparently, to TV star Roseanne Arnold, although I don't figure this out for nearly an hour. A few days earlier, she had screeched the national anthem before a professional baseball game and then grabbed her crotch. Here, at the Lawrence County Fair, the crowd makes up for a little of that disrespect by singing heartily to a brassy, static-filled soundtrack that seems to play at the wrong speed.

"We need to spread some of that patriotism around," the announcer says when it's over, and the crowd responds with thunderous applause. "Now, let's bring out those six-thousand-pound, manual-transmission, four-gears and *get it on!*"

There are nine trucks in this first class. I watch as Larry Jackson, in a '78 Chevrolet, prepares for the first pull, down on his knees in the mud, checking the connection for several minutes.

I have never seen a sport quite as silly as tractor pulling but have seldom seen people take anything more seriously. Standing out here in this empty farm country where fires burn all through the night, I begin to feel as if I have landed in another country, whose strange customs and rituals I do not yet understand.

Tractor pulling involves hooking a tractor-trailer flatbed to the back of a pickup truck and then seeing how far you can drag it. As Jackson boards his truck, those waiting behind him rev up their engines.

"How's it look?" someone asks me, coming over.

"Looks all right. Little slick."

"Little bit. You pulling?"

"Nope." He eyes the Redskins cap.

Jackson guns his engine and makes a good pull—two hundred eighty feet and two inches. A few people cheer. On the side of the waiting pickup is written "Fertilizer and Seed Company."

With each pull, the announcer repeats the same phrases over the public address system. "I believe he's got a hold of her. I believe he's got a good bite. I believe he's pulling."

The man next to me is writing down the results in a spiral notebook. I walk down the road and look out at the fields: distant fires, fog above stalks of dead corn.

"What do you say?" the man taking notes asks when I return. He's a tall, gray-haired man whose cap reads "A&S Tractor." The man with the small head is standing beside him.

"Not much."

"We haven't topped three hundred yet."

"Not yet. Maybe this one'll go."

The next truck, though, doesn't pull at all.

"I believe we have a problem," the announcer says. "I believe he has his mechanic looking it over."

"Still a little slick," the man says to me. He asks if I'm from out of the county, and I nod.

"Just stopped to see the pull," I say.

The PA squawks, and we look back out at the field: "I believe he's connected. There we go! I believe he's got the bite. I believe he's got a good pull on it."

"Looks like he's going to get three hundred," I say.

The man next to me is shaking his head. "Naw, he's pulling short. Two eighty." Indeed, the pull is only two hundred and seventy-nine.

I watch a few more pulls and leave before the next class is called. Walking in darkness back to the car, I see that the pickups are lined up for a good quarter mile now, waiting their turn for a crack at three hundred. Such are the dreams of eastern Illinois on a late summer night.

West of the fair, U.S. 50 crosses the Embarras River, so-called by French explorers who had difficulty crossing it, to Lawrenceville, where Elizabeth Reed was hung before a large crowd in 1845 for killing her husband. Next, Olney, named for a Civil War lieutenant. The story people tell about Olney isn't about war, though; it's about white squirrels. In 1902, a naturalist named Dr. Robert Ridgeway brought a pair of rare albino squirrels to Olney, Illinois, to observe their behavior. The squirrels quickly multiplied, and the town has, ever since, been overrun by them.

"Take a look in the morning," the motel clerk says. "See if you can't see some of them white squirrels."

I tell him I will and go to my room to pour a drink. A brochure there says, "Welcome to Egypt."

I have breakfast the next morning in Salem at the Little Egypt Pancake House. Before going in, I buy a copy of an oversized newspaper called *The Sentinel*, whose slogan is "Egypt's Greatest Daily." For as long as most people can remember, this area in southern Illinois has been called Little Egypt. The reason may be clear, but after I ask, I wish I hadn't. It is like asking an Indianan what *Hoosier* means.

The waitress at the Little Egypt Pancake House shrugs arrogantly. "I don't know; that's what they always called it."

An old man, seated before a plate of steaming hotcakes and sausage, seems unsettled. "What does he want to know?" he asks the waitress.

"Little Egypt."

They turn to look at me. I nod slightly.

"I'm just curious," I say.

"Well, I'll tell," says the man. "They call it Little Egypt because it reminded people of Egypt is all. There's nothing more to it than that."

"It used to tell the reason in the phone book," says the waitress. "I don't remember it, exactly, but I think it was something to do with the river that reminded people of the Nile."

"That's right," the man says.

After my breakfast arrives, I sit by the window reading the front page of *The Sentinel*, occasionally looking out at the traffic that passes back and forth on the bright pavement of Highway 50. An explanation of Little Egypt is right there in the paper. "Little Egypt: an inverted triangle of land bounded by the Ohio, Mississippi and Wabash rivers. The delta of the Ohio/Mississippi reminded immigrants of the Nile, so a city was founded there, in the 1800s, called Cairo."

Salem, a brochure says, is the "Gateway of Little Egypt." The town is built on the St. Louis–Vincennes stagecoach route and is where William Jennings Bryan lived, in a frame house on South Broadway Street. Bryan, a three-time unsuccessful candidate for president, knew well what I now begin to understand. This land is different from the East. Bryan called the East "the enemy country," because he believed it did not properly look out for the midwesterner. Beneath a statue of him in the city park, his right hand raised to make a point, Bryan's Cross of Gold speech is quoted: "You shall not press down upon the brow of labor this crown of thorns. You shall not crucify mankind upon a cross of gold."

I spend a couple of days exploring Salem, then push farther into Little Egypt, stopping in Odin, once called the "hell-hole of the Illinois Central" because of the hoodlums who would lie in wait here for the stage to come through. There's nothing much in the "hell-hole" nowadays but a silo, an antique shop and a convenience store.

The Sleeping Porch

F olks have this theory that you get the older and rarer antiques the farther east you go," Mrs. Flotta, who owns an antique shop nearby, tells me, dispelling yet another myth about the East Coast. "Not true. What they forget is that when the early settlers moved west, to Indiana and Illinois, they brought their things with them."

In Odin, the huge Lincoln Trail Antique Shop seems to sell just about everything old: antique jewelry, furniture, silverware and empty soda pop bottles. Big Chief cola, a soft drink put out by Coca-Cola years ago to compete with Orange Crush, bombed, but the empty bottles sell now for $12 apiece. I also find postcards going back to the turn of the century, a Majestic radio, victrolas, gramophones, Flexible Flyer sleds, Ipana tooth powder, a 1950s jukebox, sheet music and Big Little Books.

Also, handmade wooden, three-prong hay forks.

"That's about our biggest seller right now," Lincoln Trail owner James Soper says.

"Do those come from around here?" I ask.

"Well, no. Actually, they're from Europe. What's happened since that wall came down over there is we've been getting lots of good collectibles from Germany."

"East Germany?"

"Yes, sir. East Germany. I just got my eighth carton from East Germany. Forty-footer."

"What's the hay fork sell for?"

"Well, the hay fork's going for forty-eight dollars right now. We've also got wooden goat carts and children's sleighs."

Soper notes the burgeoning interest in antiques over the past few years. Further evidence, I think, that people want back what they gave up years ago for "progress." He says he sees more and more regular shoppers now.

"As time passes, more things we make in this country become valuable. I guess you got to let things be junk for a while first—long enough—and then they become valuable. Funny how it works."

South-central Illinois has one of the country's largest antique groups, I learn. It was organized in 1979 and has bimonthly meetings now at the Bonanza restaurant in Mt. Vernon. Mrs. Flotta says that what makes these antique shops special are "average, hard-working people. You don't see a lot of the wheelers and dealers here."

Before leaving Lincoln Trail, I buy a 1926 college yearbook that belonged originally to Pearl "Gus" Blackwell. The yearbook is full of inscriptions and ads:

Blue Ribbon Canned Goods

America's Cup of Coffee, Ask Your Grocer

M.E. Wright, Mortician, Phone 15, Night Phone 14

Home Oil Jobber

Rocke's Economy Grocery and Meat Market, Buyer of Poultry, Eggs & Cream

Morrow's Service Station, with Polarine Red Crown Accessories

The B&B Merc. Company, Phone 75

Dick's Kitchen Canners Canned Foods, "Clean—Wholesale—Economical."

At a motel in central Illinois that night, I open the musty book and take a peek into Pearl's long-ago life:

"Pearl, I sure envy you those snappy black eyes. S'pose we'll ever learn to swim?"

From Helen Buelle: "Will you ever forget the night Proctor had her fun on the sleeping porch?"

Mary Parks: "Remember the night Olga and I climbed in the sleeping porch window? Bruises! I must have the last word."

Homer T.: "Do you remember some of our rides?"

Verla: "Dear Pearl. It makes me laugh to think you want my autograph."

"Gib": "To a real pearl. A gem indeed."

Emmy Lou: "Dearest Gus. Will you ever forget our midnight marshmallow roast on the football field? And never forget the sleeping porch!"

The Biggest Walleye

J ohn McClarney, whom I met in Carlyle, has made this decision: One day he's going to catch the biggest walleye in the state of Illinois. He says it on a brisk autumn afternoon, by the rocky riprap of Lake Carlyle, on a day that has drawn dozens of fishermen to the lakefront. Barbecue smoke mixes in the air with a clean smell of lake water. Already, he's caught a green-spotted walleye and a largemouth bass, but they're small, maybe three pounds each.

I stand with him for a few minutes in the sun, beneath the perfect bright-clouded Illinois sky, as dark shadows crisscross the clear water and sudden ripples gleam. Usually, he says, he fishes on Lake Egypt. Today he's trying the state's largest lake, just off Highway 50, to see how the walleye are up here. Carlyle is a twenty-five-thousand-acre lake with a shoreline of eighty-three miles.

"They were talking about a thirty-five-pound cat the other day," he says, "so I guess that made me come up. Egypt's a great bass lake. Good striped bass. But not walleye."

"What is the biggest walleye?"

"Fourteen pounds."

"And this one's just three?"

"Yeah, but this isn't the best time of year. Crab Orchard Lake in summer, that's about the best bet."

He tells me again about the biggest walleye.

"It's like playing the lottery," he says. "I don't play the lottery. But look at the people who do, and who win the jackpots. It's never their first time. You play it long enough, spend enough money, and eventually you win."

He tosses out his jig and tries again.

Across Big Muddy

A t Ron's Lounge in downtown Lebanon, Illinois, the bartender warns me that everything changes in the western half.

"What do you mean?"

"As soon as you cross Big Muddy," he explains, "you're in the western half, and it wouldn't hurt to be prepared for it."

He's washing out glasses in the sink. A bovine man with a slight hunchback and a fleshy face that seems more female than male. I turn skeptical; he turns stubborn.

"The West doesn't start in Missouri, though," I insist. "I always thought the West began in Kansas."

"No, sir: Missouri. As soon as you cross that river out there," he says, and he points a fleshy arm toward the window, "you're in the West. You'll see."

"But not technically, not in terms of mileage."

"Sir, I'm not talking about mileage," he says, condescendingly. "I'm talking about where the East ends and the West begins. And that's it. Anyone who knows the land knows that."

"You're leaving out the Midwest, though."

He wipes off his hands and looks at me as if about to upbraid a small child.

"Sir, you can use whatever terms you want: Southeast, Northeast, Midwest. But as soon as you cross that river, you're not in the eastern United States anymore, you're in the western United States, plain and simple."

I let it go and drive on. Across a metal bridge over the muddy Mississippi. On the other side, I park and walk down to the edge of the water. It is a bright, brisk, pleasant day, but the sunlight on the river is dull, the Mississippi dirty.

Over the past decade, environmentalists have pulled more

than two hundred tons of garbage from this river, although in my imagination, the Mississippi is still as Mark Twain saw it:

> from end to end ... flaked with coal fleets and timber rafts, all managed by hand, and employing hosts of rough characters ... an acre or so of white, sweet-smelling boards in each raft, a crew of two dozen men or more, three or four wigwams scattered about the raft's vast level space for storm quarters—and I remember the rude ways and the tremendous talk of their big crews, the ex-keelboatmen and their admiringly pattering successors; for we used to swim out a quarter or a third of a mile and get on those rafts and have a ride.

There was a reason, Twain wrote, that "the muddy Mississippi water was wholesomer to drink than the clear water of the Ohio."

> If you let a pint of this yaller Mississippi water settle, you would have about a half to three-quarters of an inch of mud at the bottom, according to the stage of the river, and then it wasn't no better than Ohio water—what you wanted to do was to keep it stirred up—and when the water was low, keep mud on hand to put in and thicken the water up the way it ought to be ... there was nutritiousness in the mud and a man that drunk Mississippi water could grow corn in his stomach if he wanted to. ... You look at the graveyards; that tells the tale. Trees won't grow worth shucks in a Cincinnati graveyard, but in a Sent Louis graveyard they grow upwards of eight hundred foot high. It's all on account of the water the people drunk before they laid up.

Twain's sense of imagination seems reflected throughout the state of Missouri and is, perhaps, part of the reason the round-bodied man from Ron's Lounge was so adamant. Missouri's state roads are not numbered, as are other states'; they are lettered. Highway 50 intersects Route AA, Route ZZ and Route AB as it winds through a countryside full of cornfields and passes towns such as Freedom and Useful and even Frankenstein.

I stop in Useful to give the old Ford a rest. None of the locals, naturally, know where the name came from.

"We tried to find out," a congenial, white-haired woman named Hallie Mantle says. "But no one's been able to. So we just

Useful, Missouri, population five. None of the locals knows where the name came from.

sort of speculate. There was a church here and a post office at one time, so I imagine at some point somebody named it Useful because they figured it was a useful little stop."

Nowadays, only five people live in Useful, Missouri, and all you see driving through are two houses, the Useful cemetery and the church. The houses are antique shops. Two of the five people in Useful are Adam and Marie Bilyeu. Across the road from them, in the other old white house, lives Justice Riley.

"There were seven people in Useful when we moved here," Marie Bilyeu says. "So the population's dropped somewhat."

"That was ten years ago," her husband says.

"Most places the population goes up, but not here. We came here from Calloway County, mostly because we were so taken with this building," she says. "We expect the population to hold steady now for a while."

"What do you like about Missouri?" I ask, wondering again about the "western half."

"It's hard to explain—a certain sense of humor that no other state has. They call it the 'Show-Me State,' and that's what people expect. Nobody just accepts things here."

A few miles ahead, in California, Missouri, a city on the route of the old State Road, I stop, with the purpose of reassessing this journey. I stay for days in the California Motel, across the street from a gas station that advertises "Real Full Service," whose colored plastic triangles flutter all day in the autumn breezes and become a tiresome point of reference.

In this river country, land of explorers, where Jesse James hid out, where Daniel Boone died, I shed the journalist's skin for a while and do things just for the sake of doing them, rather than for the record. Nothing in my notebooks; all is in experience. There is one bright, summery afternoon that I paddle a canoe up the Meramec to Meramec Caverns, where there's a cool, pleasant smell of limestone and a constant, distant sound of water spilling against a cave wall. In the final room of the cave tour we sit on plastic chairs and stare at the world's largest display of cave formations—seventy feet high, seventy million years old—as the tour guide flashes colored lights on it and Kate Smith's "God Bless America" is played over the loudspeakers.

Another day, I find the picture-book, nineteenth-century German town of Hermann, beside the Missouri River. I drink beer at the Bavarian Inn and Beer Garden and hear stories about how the Big Hatchie steamboat exploded here in 1843, killing dozens of German immigrants.

Downriver on the Missouri, near the little town of Defiance, are the home and grave of Daniel Boone, who blazed the trails that helped to settle Kentucky. Missouri names celebrate Boone as much as they do Mark Twain: Boonville, Boonesboro, Boon's Lick, the Daniel Boone National Forest.

I visit the quaint town of Arrow Rock, home of George Caleb Bingham, whose paintings chronicled this transitory river country. As Bingham painted rafts and flatboats, they were being replaced by steamboats. Ironically, his town's population of eighty hasn't changed much since he lived here. Later, I stop at

Bothwell Lodge, the stone dreamhouse of John Bothwell, a prominent county attorney who once fought unsuccessfully to make the present-day Highway 50 the state road.

Without records or conclusions, I become intoxicated by the lore of the land. But one Friday afternoon when I stop at Times Beach, a deserted town near the Meramec River, just off Highway 50, the journalist returns.

Times Beach was contaminated by dioxin in the 1970s and abandoned in 1985. On one side of the bridge is a ghost town; on the other are trailers that are still occupied. One of the owners, an old man named Robert Gray, offers to tell me the story of what happened. He's dressed in a dirty white T-shirt and baggy brown slacks that ride way up his chest.

"We still get a few people come down to take a look," he says. "Don't know what they expect to see, exactly. It's almost like we're a historic stop or something they forgot to mark."

"Why did you stay?" I ask him.

"Well, economics, mostly. I couldn't afford to go."

Times Beach was contaminated, between 1969 and 1972, he says, when waste oil containing dioxin was sprayed on the roads as a way to contain the dust. The land is still contaminated, and the EPA now wants to build an incinerator and burn the soil. If that happens, they say, the area could be occupied in five or six years. The only trouble, Robert says, as we sit on the steps of his mobile home, is that the incinerator would also be used to burn contaminated soil from twenty-six other sites.

"See, it's like with that garbage out in the ocean that they had on a barge and nobody would take? Well, nobody wants contaminated soil, neither."

"So what'll happen?"

"Well, the government will win. I know that much. And the people who live here will continue to fight it. The thing I don't buy is this—they say the incinerator will be temporary. Well now, folks here aren't stupid, and a lot of them just don't believe that. Not when it's going to cost a hundred million dollars. And, of course, you tell me what that's going to do to the property values around here, having an incinerator. Do you want some lemonade?"

"Sure."

I stand in the gravel lot while he goes in and pours lemonade. His black-and-white television is tuned to a football game.

"See, there's different things that can be done," he says, handing me a dirty plastic glass. "They've talked about putting a cap on the soil and just leaving it. Well, that might be something to do. But the government's dead set on this damn incinerator. And the one thing anybody with half a mind'll tell you is you don't build an incinerator in a floodplain. But notice what I just said." He surprises me by pointing his finger in my face.

"'Half a mind'?" I repeat.

"Right. See, the government don't even have that much. Now they got this new thing, where they're saying the dioxin wasn't really as bad as they thought it was. Well, hell, I've heard some pretty good ones in my day, but that's about the topper. That's the crown." When he chuckles, his stomach rolls like ocean waves.

Marilyn Leistner, who was mayor of Times Beach in 1985, when it became "disincorporated," as she calls it, still works in the Times Beach offices, even though there is no longer a town. The story of the Times Beach contamination began, she tells me, in 1969, although it wasn't until November 1982 that a newspaper reporter notified the city that it was on a list of sites that had been sprayed with dioxin. On December 14, private testing revealed that the area was contaminated. The EPA confirmed it on December 23. "It was our Christmas message," Leistner sighs.

The federal government then bought Times Beach, using Superfund monies, and the 2,242 residents were forced to move elsewhere. Many of them sued Syntex Agribusiness Company, which was indirectly responsible for producing the dioxin. Syntex is now offering to pay for the one-hundred-million-dollar incinerator.

"I don't think people are as bitter as they used to be," Leistner says. "At this point, it's been a number of years, and we just want to see it cleaned up."

Although the government portrays Times Beach as an area that can be fixed and reinhabited in a matter of years, the story doesn't end so neatly, Leistner says.

"The feelings about the chemicals will always be there, and the stress. Whenever something goes wrong, you'll blame it on the chemicals, and you'll really never know. It's a frightening thing to happen to a town."

Leaving Missouri on Highway 50, I detour down to Whiteman Air Force Base, home to the 351st Strategic Missile Wing and one of only three bases in the country that have the Minuteman II ICBM. Out in the fields not far away are block-long missile silos, aimed at sites in the former Soviet Union. I circle the base—in this land that celebrates Boone and Bingham and Twain and James—and recognize how ineffectual Main Street's quiet rebellion really is.

Where the Bread Comes From

I t is nearly winter when the old Ford rolls into Kansas, and I feel revived again, after the wandering days in Missouri. I'm anxious to hear new stories. The tale of eastern Kansas, I learn, is that of the wheat industry. You can hear it told as well, and as often, in the old rail town of Newton as anywhere else. Newton, after all, is where Bernard Warkentin, the man credited with making Kansas "the breadbasket of the world," lived.

"You eat a lot of bread?" the tour guide at the Newton museum asks.

"As much as the next person," I reply.

"Well, then, you have Bernard Warkentin to thank."

"I do?"

"Yes, sir. Anytime you buy a loaf of bread, there's a fifty percent chance that the wheat in it came from Kansas."

"I didn't know that."

"Well. Just thank Mr. Warkentin," she says.

"I'll remember that."

Warkentin came to Kansas in 1872 and soon urged the immigration of Mennonites from Russia. The Mennonites' one hundred years of exemption from military service was ending at the time, and they began pouring into the States. Between 1874 and 1884, thousands came over to Kansas, bringing with them the Russian winter wheat seeds. So began the Kansas wheat industry.

I learn even more about Newton from Beulah Day, a feisty seventy-five-year-old who's a first-time candidate for city council. "The thing about Newton," she says, inviting me into her small living room, "is that its stories have always been fairly true. Not like Dodge. See, Newton was a cow town before Dodge was. And it was just as wild as Dodge, but the people here never played it up much.

The grave of the policeman who died in a cow town shoot-out, Newton, Kansas.

People in Dodge thought differently. They decided to commercialize it.

"Dodge has a lot of stories. But, see, if something can't be documented, I don't tell it as the truth. I tell it as something I read. There's a lot of good stories out there, but you have to tell them as stories. You can't put the truth to them unless you can prove it."

It was in 1871 that the railroad first came here, and overnight Newton became a Wild West town. "Bloody Newton is what they called it," Day says. "There were plenty of shoot-outs. There was one where a police officer named Carlos King took a gun away from a man in a dance hall. September of 1871. The man met King out on the street later and killed him with one shot. They never caught the fellow.

"The first shoot-out, though, was on Main Street. There were two cattle herders who had come up from Texas, and they got drunk and started arguing in one of the saloons. That one ended up outside too, with the men shooting each other. It turned out both of them died.

"The end of it came in 1872, after the railhead moved west to Dodge. Newton doesn't brag about it, but this was the wildest town in the West for a while."

She drives us to the Newton cemetery and shows me the grave of Carlos King. Then, again, she sets the record straight. "We were just as wild as Dodge. But the founding fathers here decided they didn't want Newton to have that kind of name. I think they're just very conservative. So you have to look around to find it. But it's there." The winds out in the cemetery are winter cold, but, telling these stories, Beulah Day doesn't seem to notice.

Johnny's Is Back

In America, you can become legendary sometimes just by calling yourself legendary. Johnny's Fruit Stand, west of Newton, is a self-made legend. After spending a couple of days in town, I have heard the ads on the radio for Johnny's maybe twenty-five times. It is always referred to as "Legendary Johnny's."

Now, heading west again on Highway 50, I begin to see the signs for it. "Johnny's Is Back" one of them reads. "Best Tomatoes In The Area, One-Half Mile," says another. "Roasted Peanuts At Johnny's—All Drivers Welcome."

Inside, there's a smell of fresh peanuts. A man by the door is stacking boxes, and I ask if he's Johnny, but he doesn't answer. A younger man offers to help me.

"Cashews," I say, and he looks toward the other man for help.

"Tomorrow I can help you," the older man says. "Today I can't."

Then, confidentially, he explains something, "The reason I let him serve you was because everyone comes in here asking for Johnny. People come in all day long saying, 'Where's Johnny? Are you Johnny?' Okay? I need to keep the other people busy too, so I don't like telling them I'm Johnny. But since you asked me, yes, I'm Johnny."

We shake hands and walk toward the cash register, where the tomatoes are. He watches as I examine them. "Tomatoes are a good buy right now. Those come from Mexico. The sorghum, though, is from right here, in Newton. You ever had sorghum?"

Turning friendlier, he lets me sample a spoonful.

"Tastes like syrup."

"You like beef jerky? That comes from right here in Newton too. You say you want cashews? Well, come back tomorrow and

Johnny, owner of "Legendary Johnny's" vegetable and fruit stand, Newton, Kansas.

I should have some in. I can't help you today. I can help you tomorrow."

I tell him I'll probably be on the road tomorrow.

"Which way you going?"

"West."

"On 50?"

"Uh-huh."

"Well, will you do me a favor?"

"What?"

"Anytime you get to a truck stop along 50, you tell them Johnny said hi. They'll know what you're talking about."

"Is that right?"

"Yes, sir. Here, in the East and all the way to Sacramento, they all know Johnny. Listen to the CB, they all mention Johnny, all the truck drivers. You have a CB? This is your major truck route, Highway 50, and this is the place that nearly every trucker stops at when he comes through Kansas. In fact, there's a group of investors that's talking to me right now. They want me to put up Johnny's Fruit Stands coast to coast."

He once had a larger, even more famous Johnny's, he tells me, down in Oklahoma. It, too, was on a truck route. Then in 1980, he had "the accident" and had to let that one go.

He says "the accident" as if I know the story and seems surprised when I have to ask. "The accident" was the thing that changed Johnny's life: a private plane crash in which the two people in the cockpit with him died—one a coworker, the other a good friend. Johnny was in a coma afterward for three months. He pulls back his shirt now and shows me the scars on his shoulder and chest. "I was all broken up. They had to put me back together again. Even when they did, they didn't know if I was going to live.

"Makes you not care quite so much about little things. I remember the plane going down. I was fully conscious and I knew I was going to die. But then I went into a coma instead. And when you're in a coma, you know you're in a coma."

"You do?"

"Well, you're maybe not aware that you're in a coma. But you're aware that you can't talk and that you can't move. You're aware that you're alive. I was aware of it for three months."

"Then you came out of it."

"Well, my brother—this is my brother here," he says, pointing to a man standing behind him who is talking on the phone. "He was always by my side, and one day he whispered, 'Breathe, Johnny, breathe,' for about twelve hours and I finally did."

When his brother gets off the phone, we shake hands.

"I knew I was going to die, that all three of us were, but somehow I came out of it, and they put my body back together again and let me live. What'd you say your name was?"

"Jim."

"So when that happened, I knew I wanted to get back in with Johnny's Fruit Stand, because this is what I love."

"When Johnny was in the hospital, all the truck drivers went out with bowls for him," Johnny's brother says.

"Fish bowls," Johnny says.

"Fish bowls, and they collected money. There were so many flowers coming in, I remember, we had to tell people to stop sending them."

"I lost a lot over that accident. Lost my money. Lost some of my friends. But you know what? The truck drivers all remembered me. I sold the big Johnny's down in Oklahoma to my sister, but I knew I wanted to get back and do this."

Johnny doesn't get too serious about things anymore; "the accident" doesn't let him.

"Listen on the CB," he says, after I pay for the tomatoes. "You have a CB? Listen on the CB, and you'll hear the truckers talking about Johnny's. All the way out to Sacramento."

Kansas Skyscrapers

T he land changes as the two-lane highway moves from the Osage Plains into the Great Plains. Hutchinson is considered the beginning of western Kansas, some say the beginning of the West itself. It's a land without trees, a rugged prairie underlaid by crumbling sedimentary rock.

Back in 1891, a national physicians' group known as the American Health Resort Association decided that Hutchinson was "the first point at which people seeking health shall stop." In a circular published that year, the group claimed, "Throughout the eastern half of the United States is found an astonishingly large number of persons whose health would be greatly improved, if not entirely recovered, and whose lives would be greatly prolonged if they just located in proper climatic surroundings."

The Health Resort Association believed that, beginning in Hutchinson and continuing into "southeastern Colorado, all of New Mexico, part of Arizona and into western Texas," the country has "the health-giving climate in longitude and latitude possessed by no other slope on earth." As loopy as this sounds, I am thinking of it as I come into Hutchinson. Perhaps what I need is this area's "health-giving climate."

To the east of the city, on the right side of the highway, are the white concrete bins of a huge grain elevator, which I recognize as the one featured on the local postcards. I turn onto Yoder Road and aim toward it through wind and dust and flakes of snow. Instead of getting closer, I seem to get farther away. I try another narrow farm road, but it's an open maze. Finally I try driving away from the elevator and, after about thirty minutes, reach it.

Blocked from the icy winds, a white-haired man stands in the doorway of the cinder-block building and watches as I stare at the tops of the bins. He seems befuddled.

"So," I say, nodding, feeling a little dumb for having come all the way out here. "The largest grain elevator in the world?"

"Nope."

"The largest in Kansas?"

He shakes his head and looks over at my car.

"That Maryland?"

I nod.

"Isn't this the one on the postcard?"

"Pardon?"

I pull the postcard from my pocket and check.

"Isn't this the elevator on the postcard?"

"Oh, it's the one on the postcard, yes," he says, and there's a hint of a smile on his face.

"But not the largest."

"No, that's right, it isn't."

We both look toward the tops of the bins, higher than the sun this early in the day.

"What it is," he says, "is the longest elevator in the world with a single head."

"A single head?"

"Yes. But people don't know what that means, so they simplify it to say it's the largest in the world. Which it isn't."

The head, he explains, is a conveyor system running across the top of the elevator. Most large grain elevators have two heads, not one.

"People'll come and look at anything if you tell them it's the largest in the world," he says, smiling, as the wind kicks up again. "If you told them it was the longest in the world with a single head, nobody'd think twice. They'd all drive right by."

The man's name is Ed Sorenson, and he's the chief engineer at this best-known, but not largest, of Kansas's elevators. The elevator, owned by the Union Equity Company, can store as much as eighteen million tons of wheat and milo at a time. Sorenson's job is to monitor the wheat and keep insects and moisture out.

He invites me into his little cinder-block office, where he explains the grain business over a cup of coffee. After a few minutes, he tells me the story of the hard red winter wheat: how it was brought here from Russia one hundred years ago and has since made this area the breadbasket of the world.

"That's interesting," I say, when he's finished.

"Most folks say so." He displays a small but satisfied grin.

Sorenson grew up in Kansas on a modest wheat and milo farm. It was always his dream to become a farmer.

"That was everyone's dream. Heck, my father did it, my grandfather did it, and it was still the dream when I was growing up. Back in the 1920s and early 1930s, it was different. You could live on an eighty-acre farm, and you could actually raise a family. Now you really need several hundred acres to get by. That's the nature of the market. There are a lot of people with two hundred, three hundred acres, and they have to work in town; they need a supplemental income. It's a lot harder to make a go now. So the dream's not so strong anymore."

By the time we walk back outside, the sun has cleared the top of the concrete skyscraper, and it hurts our eyes to look up.

"Hutchinson," he says, looking sternly at the old Ford, "is a fine place. One of the finest. I'm sure if you were interested you'd be able to find work here. Got an excellent labor pool in Hutchinson."

The coincidence of his saying this and my thinking about finding a job is surprising. As we stand there feeling the breeze, I wonder what winter will be like in Hutchinson, Kansas.

Firm Beds

The place where I stay in Hutchinson advertises "Cheap Rates, Clean Rooms," although the room I get is not clean. There are cobwebs in the corners, a dried french fry in a drawer and odd stains in the bathtub that resemble crayon scribblings.

In front of each room is an old metal chair, so, if it were warmer, you could sit with a soda or a cup of coffee and watch the traffic go by. Highway motels are modest about what they advertise, because if they weren't, people would not believe them. "Free Color TV," maybe, but seldom "Free HBO."

Along Highway 50 I see: "Free Local Calls." "Free Coffee." "Ice." "Affordable Rates." "Direct Dial Phone." "Conveniently Located." "Courteous Management." "Free Air Conditioning." "Firm Beds."

The motel is not far from downtown Hutchinson, where I go in the late afternoon to have a beer and read the classified ads. Work seems plentiful. Hutchinson is a strange blend: an old railroad town, the leading retail trade center for central Kansas, home of the National Junior College Basketball Association championships and the largest grain cooperative in the country. But "Hutch," as a man in the Main Street bar tells me, is basically a farming community.

He's a dark, gaunt fellow named Emilio, with a friendly smile and a deep voice, who makes ambulances and fire trucks. Collins Industries, where he works, is one of the major industries of Hutchinson. What he likes about Kansas, he says, "is the respect people have for one another. It's a whole lot different from the East."

"Are you from the East?"

"New Jersey," he says, and I feel a sudden kinship. "It didn't take long before I figured that people in Kansas are just a lot smarter than people in New Jersey."

"Smarter? In what way?"

"They think. They're encouraged to think."

Like many Kansas cities, Hutchinson was founded as a railroad stop. A Baptist preacher named C. C. Hutchinson picked this spot in 1872 because it was near the Little Arkansas River, and because it was just about where he thought the railroad ought to stop. Back then, towns were created on the prairie for no other reason than that every so often the train needed to stop. It's a pattern of American civilization: train station, trading post, saloons, town.

Emilio and I have two more beers. He tells me several times how great it is living in Kansas. As we drink, the streetlights come on, and then we can't see out anymore, just reflections broken only by the distant lights of vehicles crossing the wide-open spaces of central Kansas.

I go to sleep early in a bed that sags on one side and seems to have a small hard object inside the mattress on the other. I grapple with this lump repeatedly during the night. Trying to sleep, I think of Sorenson's invitation and decide this is what I'll do, start again out here in this land they call the Middle Border. It's a place to prosper quietly and to ponder the mystery of wide-open spaces. Numerous times I am awakened by the rumble of trains, which pass through downtown Hutchinson all night, just two blocks from the motel. They whistle and rattle, and their heavy smoke comes through a window that won't close.

At one point, the room fills with light and a truck engine idles outside. People talk. I hear a man say "Fuckin' A" twice. It's 2:35. There are noises afterward—bath water, hammering, television. At 4:30 I am awakened by a loud, steady moaning sound. In the room next door a bed is banging regularly against the wall, and I open my eyes to see that it's light out.

In the late Hutchinson morning, with the "health-giving climate" blowing in through the screen, not even the trains can wake me.

Out There

There's a quiet but deeply felt fear on America's Main Street. I sense it most acutely at the underground storage vaults in Hutchinson, Kansas. Six hundred and fifty feet beneath the barren wheatfields is one of the largest salt deposits in the country, three hundred and fifty feet thick, with enough salt to supply the country for a quarter million years. Adjacent to the mine are fifteen acres of underground storage bays where many of the country's most valued items are stored: government records, geophysical data, master formulas for Coca-Cola and Pepsi, master prints for thousands of motion pictures, including the original prints for *The Wizard of Oz.*

Floyd Sweet, who manages the underground vaults, says the demand for storage space has begun to exceed the supply. It is, he thinks, an ominous sign. "The reason for these vaults is very simple," he says. "They came out of the late fifties and early sixties originally. The feeling that was in the air then. The bomb scare. What people saw was that, if civilization is destroyed, it can only be rebuilt if its vital records are intact. That was the idea. If there's a nuclear war, if our civilization is destroyed, the vault has everything anybody needs to put it together again."

Sweet, a retired military man, says the vaults have grown steadily since they opened in 1959.

"What would you say if I asked to have a look?"

"What purpose?"

"Curiosity."

He shakes his head. We talk some more. Soon he changes his mind. "Okay. Just go to the mine entrance and ask for Larry Hager."

Past several sets of train tracks, there is a sloped roof with the words "Carey Salt" written on it, beneath a cold, beautiful blue sky. I pass a chain-link gateway to the loading dock, where a man is standing, apparently waiting for me.

"Larry?"

He grimaces. "Come on up. You'll have to sign a couple of forms before we can take you down."

I follow him into a large linoleum-floored, cinder-block room.

"No big deal," he says, getting me the forms. "Just agreeing that if anything happens you won't hold the company responsible."

"Happens?"

He shrugs. "Death or injury. It's just a formality."

Waiting for the elevator to come topside, Hager's eyes look over at me several times. A tall, curly-haired man, he seems to be suppressing a grin. "We had one guy," he says, "it was his first day on the job, and he took one look at that shift. His face turned green and he whipped around, says, 'Excuse me, I think I left something in the car.' We never saw him again."

He smiles at the thought. When the shift arrives—a wooden, rickety-looking, open elevator car that sways—Hager steps forward jauntily. Air blows white dust up the shaft. The door closes into darkness, and the idea of dying in this central Kansas town suddenly occurs to me. I don't hear a word he says as we drop quickly down the narrow pillar of blackness—six hundred and fifty feet in seventy seconds—in a whoosh of air that tastes of dust and salt. When it stops, we step out into the inside of the earth, where the walls and ceilings are rock and artificial light shimmers on five-foot mountains of salt.

"Hi, I'm Larry Hager," a short, hefty, bearded man says, walking up to me as the other man goes into an office.

"Oh."

We walk down a long corridor in silence. Salt glitters like diamond in the rock as we move past storage bays where boxes are filled with reels of old movies.

"So, you're looking for a job here?"

"No, I just wanted a look at the vaults. Are there any jobs available?"

"Nothing right now. But they expect something in a few weeks."

We're soon joined by a slender man named Jim Wright, who says that working here takes some getting used to.

"It's another world. Some people can handle it, some can't.

They get claustrophobic. Myself, I like the feeling down here."

"Sure, you get used to it," Hager says.

"Ever worked underground before?"

I tell him no.

Wright explains the setup: There are fifteen thousand companies that currently have information stored here, 25 percent of it film and video. There are seventeen hundred Bibles from the American Bible Company. There are also thousands of personal items like wedding dresses, diaries and stuffed pets.

"I don't know what it is," says Wright, "but the interest has definitely grown. I guess people see too many things being taken away from them."

"More and more people on top wanting to preserve things," Hager adds, "and they figure it's safe down here. Which I guess it is."

Jim Wright and Larry Hager with a ton of salt, beneath the Kansas wheat fields in Hutchinson, Kansas.

We turn a corner to a sound of engines clearing out a new storage bay. The vaults are expanding.

"Ever get any strange requests?"

"Oh, sure," Wright says. "Like we had one guy who wanted to bring down a huge stuffed moose."

"Which we would've done," Hager says, "only we couldn't fit it on the shift."

"We had one person," Wright says, "whose contract said that the only people who could retrieve his belongings were himself and Jesus Christ."

When the tour is done, we wait with several mine workers for a shift to come and take us up again. The workers push at one another, clowning in the dark elevator car, as we return to the natural light of the earth's surface.

By this time I've told Larry Hager about being on the road.

"Always wanted to do what you're doing," he says as we stand out on the loading dock, where the cold shadows of the building point across a gravel lot toward the city. "But you know what keeps me here? The people. You'll never find people as friendly as the ones right here in Kansas."

"I've heard that," I tell him.

"Hope they find a spot for you down there."

On the shady corner of Plum Street in this cattle and wheat country, I consider looking for work at the Kansas Cosmosphere, the state's major tourist attraction. I end up spending the afternoon talking about outer space.

Most of the great science museums lie on or near the country's perimeter, in big cities. The Kansas Cosmosphere is a remarkable, comprehensive space museum in the middle of winter wheat country, close to the geographical center of the United States. When I have questions about the exhibits, which include astronaut suits, rockets and illustrated histories of space travel, a teenage employee directs me to Patty Carey, the museum's founder, whose office is on the second floor.

The Cosmosphere, Carey tells me, is concerned with the role the space movement played in molding the American psyche. "What some people don't realize," she says, "is that when Kennedy made his famous speech in 1961 about landing a man

Patty Carey, in her space museum. Carey built the state's number one tourist attraction, The Kansas Cosmosphere, in Hutchinson, Kansas.

on the moon, it was a fantastic idea, considering the state of the space program at that time. We were just so far behind the Soviets then. Seven of our first satellite launches blew up. By 1961, thirty-nine percent of all our rocket launches had exploded. A man on the moon? It was almost inconceivable."

The race to the moon and the turnaround of the American space program gave the country a new sense of optimism, Carey believes. Anything was possible. It changed the way Americans think.

Carey was a housewife, she says, in 1962, when she developed the first planetarium in Kansas, here in Hutchinson. "It was a barn, really, out by the fairgrounds. Home to many pigeons." In 1981, enlisting the help of Max Airy, a planetarium director from Texas, she began to seek funding for the Cosmosphere. She did so, she says, because she was "convinced of its importance."

"Space always struck me as this great metaphor, what lies 'out there.' I guess you could say we were naive. We didn't know we couldn't do it. So we did.

"When I was a girl, I'd go out in the yard every evening and look at the stars. I always wanted to go to the moon, and I guess I was a little disappointed when they saw the other side of it, because I liked that little bit of mystery."

Talking with Patty Carey, I feel like staying in Hutchinson even more. It is a place that tugs at you. Not quickly. A little bit each day, telling you about itself, making you want to spend another night to hear some more.

Days from Another Season

E ven in the worst weeks of winter, there are days that belong to other seasons, warm afternoons that confuse the fauna and flora. One such day occurs in the bitter winter of Hutchinson. The old Ford is running well, so that morning I decide to go exploring, heading south.

The dirt road to Robert and Velma Schrock's house is marked by horse-and-buggy tracks. Past scrubby fields where, in summer, wheat and milo grow, I drive through the Amish community of Yoder. Hand-painted signs appear on the lawns of old white wooden houses: "Eggs For Sale," "Vegetables" and "Quilts."

The journey feels right; there are no misgivings. When I stop at the Schrocks' old farmhouse, a little boy on a donkey comes over and circles the old Ford. His father, Robert Schrock, is in the doorway of a big red barn, wearing jeans and a denim coat with no buttons. As he greets me, two lambs run up and sniff tentatively at my pants. There is a sign by the road saying the Schrocks seek a part-time farmhand, and I decide to apply. We look at each other's beards for a while, and then he leads me to their guest house.

"We can give you a try in the morning," he says. "Day starts early, though, and it's a long one. Don't know if you'll care for this type of work."

"I'm willing to give it a shot," I say.

"Well. Don't know if you'll like it."

The lambs run alongside as we walk beneath the bare trees.

"Now you just make yourself at home here," Robert Schrock says. "And you're going to want to get plenty of rest, because the day is long."

Inside the guest house are an icebox and a propane lamp. Over the wood stove, a painting depicts an Amish buggy heading into the shade of a covered bridge. On the opposite wall is the Lord's Prayer and a sign, "Welcome to Our Farm."

After Robert Schrock leaves me, I light the lamp and sit for a while at the kitchen table with my notebook, as the cool evening light comes in through the screen, bringing the smell of animals and a sound of peacocks screeching at one another.

The Amish, I learn from Robert Schrock, came to Kansas in the late nineteenth century and settled in small groups. Yoder is a community of forty Amish families now, named for Eli Yoder, the original settler. The Amish here are Old Order—they seek to live as their ancestors did, with no electricity, no telephones and no automobiles. They're left alone; they trade with one another. It's rare that they take in non-Amish, and I sense they are reluctant about having me.

I sit and listen to the faint stirring in the tree branches and the metal flaps of a hog feeder clacking. When I go back outside, it's nearly dark, and a candle is burning in the harness shop where there are several buggies—a coach, one-seaters and the traditional two-seaters.

I walk to where Schrock is working and offer to help.

"Don't know what you could do right now," he says and looks around. Finally, he instructs me to stack the harnesses for him.

Robert Schrock was born down the road, forty-two years ago. He has spent his life here in Yoder. He married a Yoder girl, he says, and has tried to live the way God intended him to live.

"Somewhere," he says, as he lifts the harness off a horse and rubs the sore spot on the animal's hide, "people just got off the track, near as I can tell. And they hasn't gotten back on it. Trying to get a lot of other folks off the track too."

When Schrock closes up the barn, it's dark, and we lean up against a buggy wheel beneath a sky full of stars and listen to the wind. I sense that he really doesn't want help. He wants to talk. He wants company in his isolated world of farm animals and family and barren wheatfields.

"It's funny," I say, "the contrast between the space museum up in Hutchinson and a place like this."

"Well," Schrock says, and it's a long time before he speaks again. "I can't say I think much about having men walking up there on that moon."

The Amish community of Yoder, Kansas.

"It's hard to believe we did it."

"Well." His silence seems a suppression of anger. "Every time I think about it, I just wish they hadn't done it."

"Walk on the moon?"

"It's tampering with something that we shouldn't have been tampering with," he says. "Every time I hear about them sending up one of those spaceships, it makes me mad. And every time, it seems like something goes wrong with the weather. You can almost count on it."

"The weather?"

"That's right."

We listen to the sound of the horses whinnying in the dark. Moonglow lights the fields, but beneath the trees, it's hard to see his face. It surprises me when I do—his Amish features and the beard with a shaved upper lip, the Amish symbol of marriage. Across the yard, a faint yellow light falls from the kitchen window, where, I can see, his family is seated around the table, eating.

Although the Amish buy and sell from one another, the

difficult economy has forced them recently to sell to outsiders. The next day, as I help Robert Schrock repair a buggy, several non-Amish people come by. He works late again, by candlelight, but won't let me help. Mostly, I stand and listen. Several times, up at the intersection, buggies pass, making a steady clop-clop-clop sound in the dirt.

The bed in the Schrocks' guest house is huge. In the middle of the night, peacocks screech, and the moonlight is refracted in the old glass of the windows. I wake to the sound of roosters. The Schrocks get up before six each day, so I am up then too. Beside the barn, a pony is running around in circles, full of energy; there's a good smell of earth in the morning shade, as moisture rises and light spreads among the farm buildings.

I walk down the long, quiet road, feeling the cool sunlight on my face. An Amish woman hanging clothes looks as I pass her house, but she doesn't wave, doesn't smile.

Back at the Schrocks', Robert's wife Velma has brought me breakfast. Robert, I see, silhouetted in the harness shop, is hitching up a horse.

"Awfully peaceful out here," I say.

"Yes," she says, "although there's a lot of work to be done. You want coffee?"

"No, thanks. Do you have milk?"

"We do have milk," she says, "but it's pure milk. Probably not what you're used to."

She brings me eggs and bread, and it's delicious in the cool moist morning. When the milk comes, it's in a glass with ice cubes. At one point the two lambs come up and watch me eat.

Outside, Robert Schrock has a buggy hitched up again and seems impatient. "Need to take some eggs down the road," he says finally, coming to the guest house but not looking at me. "You can join me if you want to." I climb up into the buggy with him, and he shakes the reins. The horse begins to trot, steadily, the wheels crunching in dirt, until we get to an intersection, where Schrock pulls the rein and we turn to the right.

"No shock absorbers on this," I say.

"Don't see why you'd need any," he says.

We ride on in silence. At the other farm, I wait in the buggy as the horse chews on scrub grass and Schrock carries a tray of eggs. Riding back, he tells me how he needs to build a new workshop.

By the third morning, I know I'm in the way and tell them I have decided to leave. Robert Schrock nods. Velma asks where I'm heading.

"Just traveling," I say.

"Well, I hope you find someplace where you're happy."

A depressing thought, put that way. The Schrocks, like families all along America's Main Street, are happy for what they have preserved: a way of life that has not been touched by progress. I drive down these unspoiled dirt roads back toward the routes that were designed for motorized travel.

Cow Town

The wind is cold and gusty as the road comes to Dodge City, Kansas, on the route of the old Santa Fe line. The Santa Fe was the railroad that, in many ways, opened up the West—stopping at Newton in 1871, Hutchinson in August 1872 and Dodge in September that year, civilizing a land that explorer Zebulon Pike in 1806 had called "uninhabitable desert." It's still the more uncivilized aspects of the region, though, that people like to celebrate.

For a while, when Dodge was the westernmost of the Kansas cow towns and a major shipping point for Texas cattle, it had the nickname "Hell on the High Plains." The lawless period lasted only about three years, but the town still shamelessly promotes those Wild West years with shows and museums and a re-created Front Street.

No longer lawless, Dodge is obviously still a cow town. A place where men dress in boots and cowboy hats, where cattle horns are mounted over doorways and portraits of steers hang on office walls. Cattle is the leading industry here, with two of the largest slaughterhouses in the world just down the road. All night and day, trucks full of cattle move up and down Wyatt Earp Boulevard, which is what Highway 50 is called in Dodge.

If you really want to see cattle, though, the woman at the Silver Spur lounge says, you'd best go to the auction.

"There's an auction?"

"Largest cattle auction in the world. Up at Winter Livestock. Every Wednesday."

Before I stop at the auction, I visit a western wear shop to buy a cowboy hat. The selection and the range of prices are enormous. I tell the clerk I'm looking for a "basic" cowboy hat, and he doesn't seem to understand.

"Nothing fancy, nothing too expensive."

He finally selects for me a black hat with a wide brim for thirty-five dollars.

At Winter Livestock, I park the old Ford among the dozens of pickup trucks. Inside, I adjust my hat and saunter over toward the garbled sounds of the auctioneer. I like the freedom of not being me.

Pushed as close to the auction box as possible, I still find it nearly impossible to understand the auctioneer, although I see that he is selling off calves, and there is no shortage of bids.

I'm soon nudged by a very heavy man with one arm. "At's buying," he says, looking down at me. "Your cattle gonna come in clear. This here feeder."

"Feeder?"

"Yes, sir, come up f'another. 'At's buying to next hour your feeder."

"Next hour, you say?"

"Hour, two, yes, sir."

He nods cordially and turns. I move to put some distance between us and stand by the fence with a group of middle-aged cowboys: professional buyers. Although I'm not interested in buying a steer today, the excitement of the auction, of all the people gathered on a brisk afternoon, is intoxicating. Standing beside these men, I adjust my hat several times and absently kick at the dirt, acting as if I belong here and just don't have anything to say at the moment. Their breaths are all visible in the raw Kansas air. A tall, skinny woman in jeans and a sleeveless down jacket is over by the fence, smiling at me I think.

The sun is very bright, and there's a strong stench of cattle and manure. I look up and the woman is standing next to me now, gesturing with an unlit cigarette.

"You're not no buyer," she says.

"How can you tell?"

"Come on," she says. "You're not no buyer."

I pull on the brim of my cowboy hat. "I didn't know it was so obvious."

"What are you doing if you're not no buyer?"

She seems too intent on this point. Arc there auction police here to weed out the nonbuyers, the fakers?

"Well, what about you?" I say. "You're not a buyer, either, are you?"

She laughs quietly and turns away. Her thin arms fold easily over her stomach, and I sneak a glance at her—a long, pale face with freckles. Pigtails. Unlit cigarette held out still.

"Looking for m'girlfriends," she says with a sudden twang.

As we stand there, she mumbles—"Good one," "A lot of hamburger there," "Forget it, partner"—but never speaks directly to me, until finally she surprises me by twisting around and extending her hand. "My name's Janice."

We shake.

"Your name?"

"Jim."

"What you ought to do, Jim, you ought to come back during rodeo time."

I tug on the hat brim again. It becomes a convenient mannerism.

"They got some bulls here like you never seen, Jim. Like Crooked Nose. 'Course that's sort of a legendary one. Only got one horn, but very smart. You know, once you get out so many times, you don't take the fake no more."

As we squint up at the auction box, Janice nervously shifts her weight from leg to leg and waves a few times at people in the crowd, although I don't see anyone wave back.

"Where are you from, Jim?"

I tell her I'm from the East, but now I'm just out wandering, that I have no destination. It makes her smile.

"That's funny," she says.

"No, it's true."

"Where are you staying, Jim?"

"Silver Spur."

She looks me over again, disbelieving, pointing with the cigarette. "Now, we're going to stop in Silver Spur tonight, Jim. If you're there, maybe I'll see you."

A few moments later, she shakes my hand good-bye and gives me a wide smile. Later, shortly before I leave, I see her talking to a couple of chubby old cowboys, gesturing wildly with the unlit cigarette. The cowboys are all laughing.

Behind the spirit of Dodge is an aggressive belief that this town is truer than others; that the natives possess a sense of independence not seen in other places. In some people, it seems deeply felt; in others, just strongly defended.

At the Silver Spur, a man with a seven-gallon hat asks how I like Dodge.

"Just fine," I say.

"Business here?"

"No."

"Tourist?"

"Not really."

He takes off the hat and frowns.

"Well, what's that leave?"

"Just driving through."

"Okay."

A second man takes his hat off too. He's smaller and stockier, though both of these men are big in Dodge. The three of us hold our hats in our right hands.

The first man is George Heinrichs, who owns the Silver Spur. The other is Ron Long, former rodeo rider and deputy marshal.

"I've heard about the rodeo," I tell him.

"Not many people who haven't."

"That's the truth," Heinrichs adds.

"I'll tell you one thing," says Long. "You drive anywhere in this country, you'll never find another place that has the spirit this town has. And what it is is the spirit of the cowboy. Everybody who comes through Dodge, they come here looking for it. Why? Well, because the cowboy punches no clock. The cowboy comes and goes as he pleases. People still yearn for that.

"Now, I can tell you a story or two about Dodge," he says, and Heinrichs chuckles. "If you have a minute."

"He'll tell you more stories than you want to hear," Heinrichs says.

"I'll tell you a little story about cattle," he says, motioning for us to sit down.

One can almost feel the hooey gathering.

"'Course, there's more cattle here, you realize, than there is anywhere else. By far. Certainly more than in Texas. I don't care if anybody tells you different."

Heinrichs winks at me.

"But let me tell you this story about it," Long goes on, carefully setting down his hat. "Back in eighty-four, you may recall, they had the Republican National Convention down in Dallas. And, why, they had us bring down some Kansas longhorn steers for it. You know, they took pictures of the steers with the Dallas skyline in the background and all that. Well, I was down there wearing my old-fashioned outfit, like I do, and this lady, why, she was telling me how it was the greatest thing that ever happened to Texas. How finally people were going to see the real Texas. All this bull. She was laying it on real heavy about the real Texas and the longhorn cattle and all, and then she said, 'Where are you from?' and I said, 'Why, Dodge City, Kansas.' She said, 'Oh, what are you doing here?' I tilted my hat up and said, 'Well, they apparently didn't have enough big steers here in Texas, because they had to call up to us to bring some down. We brought down forty-five head of big steer for the convention.' And, God, she went down just like a balloon when I said that."

Heinrichs and Long immediately break into raucous laughter, and I feel obligated to join them. When it stops, Long lifts his hat and stands. "Well, now, listen," he says. "You going to be in town for a while, drop by, because I've got something I'd like to show you. Something I think you'd like to see."

Heinrichs winks again as Long goes out. But once Long is gone, he surprises me. "One thing about Dodge," he says, "you'll see a lot of people who wear the boots and the western wear. But Ron Long, now, he's a real cowboy. Not all of them are." The way he looks out the door down Wyatt Earp Boulevard, he could just as easily be talking about some renowned gunslinger who had just come into town after bringing cattle up the Chisholm Trail.

In Dodge, as in any town that thrives on tourism, there is a core group of people who makes sure that the right things are said. One of them used to be Raymond House, the marshal of Dodge, a colorful man who for many years was Long's best friend. The two haven't spoken in years, I learn, and people in Dodge have their theories about it. Some say it's just a matter of personalities; others, that House is bitter about losing full marshal status a few years back. House, several people say, used to be the best storyteller in Dodge, but he's quit telling. When I stop in the marshal's office to meet him, he is cool to me. He says he has nothing to say about Dodge City.

So I go over to see Ron Long, whose office is a half block off Wyatt Earp, at the roofing company he owns. "Come on in," he says, obviously pleased to see me. "Come right in. Feel free to look at any of the pictures on the wall." The "pictures" are framed photographs of Long with various dignitaries including John F. Kennedy and J. Edgar Hoover.

"The one you're looking at," he says, indicating a photo on the wall, "was when John F. Kennedy was campaigning and, why, we presented him with a cowboy hat. May be the only picture of him ever taken with one. American Hat Institute wrote and wanted to get a copy of that.

"It's a funny thing too, because he went from here down into Texas and they presented him with a hat, but he wouldn't put it on for the pictures." Long chuckles and shakes his head at the plight of the poor Texans.

We look at several other pictures, and he tells me stories about his rodeo-riding days, about the auction and about the spirit of Dodge: a place where deals are still made on just a handshake.

"Now, this," he says dramatically, guiding me to a corner of his office, "is what I wanted to show you." His eyes turn to a familiar-looking Marlboro cigarette magazine ad, with a cowboy roping a steer. The ad is framed on his wall.

"You recognize that?"

I've seen it in magazines.

"Do you recognize it?"

"I think so."

He's watching me closely, timing his delivery.

"Why, that's my steer they used in the advertisement."

He stands back. We stare for several moments at the Marlboro ad.

"Shot it just south of Dodge there and they used my steer. Renamed him Marlboro Red right after that come out."

He hands me several other pictures of Marlboro Red before walking with me outside. I hear him chuckling again as I unlock the old Ford.

"Now, there's an example," he calls from the porch.

"Pardon?"

"You rarely see people around here locking their cars. That's how I had you pegged for an easterner."

He stands there grinning as I open the door and drive off into the sunset.

Trail Ruts

In Dodge, I count what's left in the tackle box and see it's half of what it once was. I take a few bills and wander down to the Silver Spur lounge, wondering how soon this journey will come to an end.

Janice arrives at ten, with two other women, bringing the cold smell of outdoors, of leather and of liquor. One of the women is big and pudgy, wearing a white blouse that's too tight and a brown leather jacket. The other is short and sturdy. All three have on jeans and cowboy boots.

"Hey, there," Janice says, and she nudges me with her elbow as she sits down.

"This is Mo," she says. "And this is Gretchen, Jim."

Mo nods, Gretchen looks away. We order beers.

"Mo and I are thinking of opening up an authentic western wear shop, Jim."

"In Dodge?"

"We're thinking of it. You interested?"

She looks me over again, her eyes blue, her face freckled, chewing gum a little dopily. And then suddenly she leans forward and whispers, "I don't really know them too well," nodding toward the other two, who are talking. "Although Mo and I have been hanging around together. You know."

"Sure."

After the beers arrive, Janice points her unlit cigarette at me and seems about to speak, but she's actually looking at two men who have just walked in. Handsome cowboys. Out in the parking lot, seven men are leaning against the sides of their cars, watching traffic. All seven are wearing cowboy hats.

"So tell me about Dodge," I say.

"Well, there's a lot I could tell you, Jim." She gets tired of fingering the cigarette and puts it behind her ear. "I'm no expert—um, did anyone tell you about the trail ruts?"

"No."

"The bullet holes?"

"Nope."

"Well, that's in Cimarron."

"Want to go take a look at them?" says Mo, the hefty woman, speaking to Janice. Mo and Gretchen stare at us for a moment, with droopy eyes. They seem very bored.

"Yeah, let's do that," Janice says.

"What are the bullet holes?"

We finish our beers, and I pay the tab. Outside, they're all three squeezed in the front of Janice's white pickup. The engine is clicking loudly, the radio playing Johnny Cash.

"Hop in," Janice says.

"Your truck ought to get together with my Ford," I say.

"Hun?" She drives too fast into the night west of Dodge. The land is bright but foggy under the full moon.

First stop, the trail ruts. Northwest of Dodge, adjacent to Highway 50, 140 acres have been preserved as national parkland, marking the path of the Santa Fe Trail. Janice parks, and we walk out into the fields. Indentations made 150 years ago by wagon and mule teams that passed through en route to Santa Fe are still visible. In western Kansas and into Colorado, Highway 50 traces the most important of the trade routes west, a course determined by William Becknell. Becknell left Franklin, Missouri, in September 1821 with a pack train of goods and returned to Missouri weighed down with a fortune in silver coin. Missourians quickly followed his example, loading wagon trains with cotton, silk and hardwood. New Mexico, having won its independence from Spain, was anxious for American goods, and trade on the Trail soon became a half-million-dollar-a-year business. In 1825, Congress approved the marking and surveying of the Trail, making it one of the first "roads" in the West. The Santa Fe Trail lasted half a century, until the railroad made it obsolete. Later, it became a stagecoach trail and, much later, a highway.

Three of us walk far enough into the fields that the lights from Wyatt Earp are no longer visible. Mo stays by the edge of the road, trying unsuccessfully to light her cigarette. The wind is icy and hard and makes a howling sound.

"Better go," Janice says, her teeth chattering.

On Main Street, Cimarron, she parks by A Street.

"Looks like the 1930s," I say of the old brick town.

"That's the courthouse there," she says, walking toward a building on the corner beside a secondhand store. "And these are the bullet holes."

The story of the Cimarron bullet holes has to do with one of the more legendary of county seat wars, I learn. County seat wars were common in the 1800s, when new towns went up on the prairie every few weeks. The battle here was between Cimarron and Ingalls, a town to the west that was built around an irrigation system. The founders of Ingalls sought to create the agricultural center of the Midwest and took it upon themselves to make Ingalls the county seat of Ford County. But Cimarron already claimed that distinction and refused to give up its records.

Early in 1889, residents of Ingalls came to Cimarron to steal the records. Their plans were indiscreet, though, and Cimarron stationed gunmen all over the downtown. The Ingalls men rode in from the northwest and up Main Street to this building with the bullet holes. A riot ensued; many were wounded, and one man was killed. Afterward, the records were peacefully turned over to Ingalls, although the irrigation ditch soon went dry, and the population dwindled to one hundred. In 1893, an election was held, and Cimarron again became the county seat, which it remains today. The bullet holes from that day in 1889 are still there. You can feel them in the bricks.

Going back, we pass farmland and cattle pens, signs that read "Eat Beef, Keep Slim." Over the rattle of the engine and the whining of the belts when she brakes, Janice suggests that we name convenience stores.

"Name them?" I say.

"Okay," Mo says. "Dart In."

"Loaf and Jug," Janice says.

"Quick Stop. Dash In. Quick Shop," Mo says.

"United Dairy Farmers," Gretchen says.

"Shore Stop," Mo says.

"7-Eleven," I offer.

"How many is that?"

"Eight," says Gretchen. "We had eleven the other day."

We drive back into Dodge much too fast, thinking about convenience stores. When a Dolly Parton song comes on the radio, Mo turns up the volume and sings along, her leg moving furiously against mine, the engine knocking and kicking.

"Hey," Janice calls after she lets me off. "I'll try to come by tomorrow."

What keeps me in Dodge is the enthusiasm of the people and the cheap price of hooey. People treat visitors like cowboys who have wandered in from the prairie and just want to have a little rest and relaxation. The idea of staying is, again, tempting. A man in the Silver Spur says he'll gladly take me on a cattle drive once spring comes around. Ron Long assures me he can even get me into the rodeo next September if I'm interested. But the greatest lure comes from Dale Northern, the mayor, who offers to make me a marshal of Dodge City.

The Mayor of Dodge

H appy hour, Friday afternoon. There are snowflakes in the dreary winter wind.

"Let me buy you a drink," Dale Northern, the mayor of Dodge, says when he finds that I'm a visitor. He motions to the bartender, who sets us up.

Northern is a peppy, silver-haired man in his sixties who sold cars before he became mayor. Now, he says, he sells Dodge. "One thing about this town is people have their own way of doing things. It's like, when I run for mayor, I just win. I've never taken any money for my election, nor have I ever asked anybody to vote for me. In fact, each time I run I tell people not to vote for me, because I don't really want to be elected. But they vote for me anyway. They figure I must be honest if I tell 'em I'm not worth voting for. So it's sort of a funny situation. But what can I do? They keep electing me, I've got to serve."

He pauses only long enough to sip his drink. "I love bars," he says. "I used to keep my office in one. Place called the Cowtown.

"'Course, most people don't really understand Dodge. They've heard of it, but they don't know what to expect. A lot of them think when we get a little low on money out here, we hold up trains or something. Some folks aren't even sure what state we're in. Some think we're in Texas somewhere.

"I was in St. Louis once, and I got a cab to the airport and the guy was showing me his tilt steering wheel. He was making it go up and down, like we didn't have anything like that in Dodge. I just said, 'Boy, that suuuure is pretty.' I don't think he got it, though."

"There are still a lot of storytellers here, aren't there?" I ask.

"Well, some. You grow up hearing stories, and you end up telling them. It takes a pretty long while before you're sure what

Dale Northern, the mayor of Dodge City, Kansas.

to believe. I'm not sure yet. I think that's a condition of this part of the country. It's just sort of a pastime.

"When I was a boy, I remember they told me about the gold being here. 'Course, Coronado came through searching for the lost city of gold in 1541. But I must've got the dates wrong, because I grew up thinking I could find it in the 1930s."

He laughs. I do too, more at his laugh than at what he's saying. Several people, I see, are leaning in, listening. He rubs his hands together several times as if he's cold, although it's warm in the bar, almost hot. Outside, the snowflakes are coming thicker in the streetlights along Wyatt Earp Boulevard.

"People like to have fun with it," he says, "and I'll be the first to say I'm no different. It's like when I went into the Silver Spur recently and there were these two guys there from Canada. I'd never seen them before, so I go up to them, and I say, 'Hello, my name is Dale Northern and I'm the mayor of Dodge City.' I'll do that with anybody who comes through Dodge.

"Well, I'm sitting there having a drink, and I can tell right away they don't believe me. They think I must be some kind of weird guy. Some kind of nut. You know, the mayor wouldn't be sitting there by himself, having a drink.

"So a few minutes later, I go over and say, 'Did you buy the story about the mayor?' And they said, no, they hadn't.

"So I say, 'Well, okay, listen, I lied to you. I'm actually the marshal of Dodge City.' Which I am. And they just looked at me again. So I left them alone for a few more minutes."

Northern takes a long drink. It's for effect. There's an audience now, a semicircle around him. He rubs his hands together again, warming them for the finale.

"And so, then, I finally go over again, kind of shaking my head and say, 'Did you buy the marshal story?' And they said, 'No, not really.' 'Well, I lied to you again,' I said, and I kind of looked down like I was feeling guilty for it." He rubs his hands together vigorously.

"'I've actually been out of work for five years and I just told you all that to impress you. But I hope we can still be friends.'

"It had started to rain outside and these guys had their truck parked up a few blocks at Boot Hill Cemetery. So eventually they asked if I could give them a lift. Well, all I had with me was my two-seater, so I said, 'I don't have enough room in my Corvette, but if you wait, I'll get my chauffeur to come and pick you up.'"

As Northern drinks again, I realize that this is no longer a story he's telling just me; my presence seems barely to matter now.

"Well, we all just laughed at that," Northern says, "but before I left I said to the bartender, 'Hold these guys here if you can.' And I came right back there in the limo. I was sitting in the back seat watching television and they opened the door and I just said, 'Hi there.'"

The audience bursts into laughter. "Are you married?" he asks me, when it finally stops.

"Not yet."

"Why?"

"Tough question."

"Well, now let me tell you about that." The hands rub. "Main problem with getting married is your wife won't let you act like a big shot anymore. I remember one time when I was out in Los Angeles to make Johnny Carson a marshal of Dodge. Afterward, my wife and I go to this restaurant to eat. Well, there's this big line to get in and I start thinking, 'Heck, here I am, mayor of Dodge City. I just made Johnny Carson a marshal. I shouldn't have to wait for a table.' My wife's saying we've got to wait just like everyone else, but I keep figuring they'll be impressed enough when they find out who I am to maybe get us in a little quicker.

"So I go up to the maitre d' and I tell him I'm the marshal of Dodge City. He just looks at me for a moment, then he says, 'Oh, that's all right, sir, my brother's a police officer too, and he always feels safe in here.'

"Well, my wife, she just looks at me and shakes her head. 'So what are you going to do now, big shot?'"

In the darkened bar, as snow fills the night sky, the crowd roars.

In the parking lot Dale Northern offers to make me a marshal of Dodge City.

"You just come around my office during the day, and we'll do the whole ceremony," he says. "I think you'd make a fine marshal of Dodge."

Before riding off on his motorcycle, the mayor asks if I'd like to hear "this philosophy I've got." Thick flakes of snow are sticking to our faces and clothes. I can barely see him.

"Sure," I say.

"It's worked for me and maybe it'll be of some use to you. Always try to associate with people you can learn something from. Not people who are the same as you or are not as well off as you, but people who know more than you or can do something better than you can. Because they'll teach you. You go through life with that philosophy and you can't help but be a winner."

We shake hands heartily in the snow as cattle trucks go back and forth on the sopping highway. The first real snow of this journey is thick, settling on the lawns.

I sit in the Silver Spur for a while with bourbon, watching the snow fall and thinking about Dale Northern's advice and his offer. I feel more welcome in Dodge City, Kansas, than I have anywhere else on this trip, and I decide to stay for a while. Dodge: where the hooey is as thick as the snow and just as insulating.

Snow stays on the ground for several weeks in central Kansas. The winds are bone chilling, and on the brightest afternoons water trickles down the drain outside my window. At dawn, there are often fresh icicles hanging from the ledge and a bracing air on the edges of the room.

Eventually, Dodge becomes too familiar, its people too accepting. A faint silver light glows up out of the glistening, barren wheatfields. I am driving the old Ford west on Wyatt Earp, past a sign reading "Eat Beef," when I decide, again, to go, to keep going, afraid that if I linger much longer, I will miss what lies ahead. Trucks and campers pass me on this two-lane road into the prairie.

A hundred years ago, when the eastern sky lit the morning, it revealed the shapes of bison grazing shoulder to shoulder. For the Cheyenne and Kiowa, bison (incorrectly called buffalo) were life itself—food, shelter and clothing. After the "fire horse" came through, most of the bison were slaughtered. The only ones left now are at refuges. There's a large refuge in the sand dunes south of Garden City, thirty-seven hundred acres set aside for the animals to graze. Several of them look up as I drive by in the moist early morning. Then they go back to what they were doing.

Water Tower Towns

T heir names are not on signs beside the highway but on water towers in the grainfields. I stop in one of these towns called Holcomb and remember the story of Dick and Perry and the crime that, some say, changed central Kansas forever. The murder became the basis for Truman Capote's *In Cold Blood.*

Terry Bontrager tells me that her earliest childhood memory is that day in 1959 when she found out that her neighbors, the Clutter family, had been killed. For weeks, she says, people didn't know what to believe. They suspected someone from Holcomb had done it.

"Right after it happened, Dad went out and got the biggest lock he could find. We'd never had locks before. Nobody locked their doors. I was twenty-two years old before I could stay by myself again. It just didn't make any sense. The Clutters didn't have any money in their house. They were killed for nothing."

Ron Long, who also grew up in the area, had told me: "That one thing, more than anything else, changed this region. People who'd never locked their doors all of a sudden did. It was a while before they knew who did it, and that whole time nobody trusted one another. That was the real damage it did. I was up there and saw the pictures of poor Herb with his throat cut. You don't forget something like that."

Genevieve Hertel, a librarian: "The killings had a very, very strong impact. Then, I think, people wanted to put it behind them, to forget it. But I don't know that they have."

I drive down to the old Clutter farm on a nippy, windswept afternoon. The ground is hard and bare, and I just stare out at the land, as people still sometimes do. Eventually a car comes down the narrow farm road and stops. A man steps out. Lately, a lot of strangers have been moving to this area to work in the beef-processing plants, and the natives are sometimes suspicious.

"What's up, pal?" this man asks me, hitching up his trousers.

"Just looking."

"At what?"

"The farm."

"Well, you better move on now."

His wife is in the car, and she glares at me. They stay parked, watching, as I drive off, not sure who I am but making sure I don't come back.

Up the road in Lakin, time has changed again. The clerk at a small grocery store asks if I know I've just passed into mountain time. "Congratulations," she says, "you gained an hour."

An old rail town, Lakin advertises itself this way: "Bird watching and people watching can be enjoyed, with an abundance of local species to be seen."

But as I drive down Buffalo Street, past the county museum, I see only birds. Then I find out why. All of the people are gathered out in front of the post office. There's no reason for it I can discern other than today is Saturday and that's what people do in small Kansas towns on Saturday. They park their trucks in front of the post office and talk to one another.

I stop in Lakin overnight, carrying with me Dale Northern's philosophy and wearing my cowboy hat.

Colorado Kool Aid

nother spring is in the air as I reach Colorado. The prairie breeze carries a warm scent of early wildflowers.

The first town in Colorado is Holly, on the mountain branch of the Santa Fe Trail. Holly was named for Hiram Holley, a settler who staked a claim for a cattle ranch on the Trail back in 1871. His stone barn, the first structure in Holly, still stands several blocks off Highway 50. "I use it to store things right now," Bill Wilson, who owns the old Holley ranch, tells me. "One of these days, I may look into getting it on the National Register. But it's not a high priority thing with me." Wilson, forty-nine, is a rancher who takes care of cattle, grows a few crops and programs computers. Such is the changing Midwest.

On a surprisingly warm afternoon, cars queue up outside a grandstand on the edge of Holly, and, although I see no announcement of what it is they're going to see, I join in. A passive adventurer gets in lines.

A small sign by the gate at last explains: "Rodeo." But after I park and pay the dollar admission, I see that it is actually a horse race. The Colorado and American flags flap above the racing board in the dusty wind while Tammy Wynette sings through the loudspeakers. Cowboy boots are tapping.

A voice breaks in on the music. "Be sure and visit the concession stand. Also, the Beer Shack's open, and they've got that Colorado Kool Aid down there—Coors. And this year, they've also got wine coolers. So if wine coolers suit your fancy, well, then, be sure and visit the Beer Shack. The Beer Shack's located next to the west side of the grandstand."

It sounds like a good suggestion. I go over and buy a beer, then put down a five-dollar bet on Dusty Action to win in the third. At post time, I line up with everyone along the fence in the sun to squint out at the scrubby field. Dusty Action finishes last. People drop their tickets and flip through programs. On to the fourth.

Back by the betting windows, a man, noticing my hesitation, takes my program and studies it. He seems to be the only man at the track not wearing a shirt. "I'll tell you the best one to go on," he says. "Right here, okay, you've got a seven to two. Those are going to shift by post time, to maybe four to one. Now that's a good horse right there, Wise Evidence. Put five dollars down."

He's a very large man with tousled hair and a dirty belly; his eyes are slits. "See how it goes. Comes in at four to one, you pick up fifteen extra dollars." I put five dollars on Wise Evidence, as he suggests, and we go for more beers.

"Listen, my man," he says, walking back toward the fence. "I'll show you how you can tell beforehand which horse has the advantage."

He leads me to the stable area, walking with a quick, cocky cadence unusual in such a large man, to where the six horses for the next race, a five-furlough, are being primed.

"That's my man Schwartz there," he says, as we get to the fence, indicating, I guess, the jockey. "With him, Big Boy Lost is a good bet on this race."

The horse he indicates suddenly bucks and pulls at the reins. "But take a look there. Pester. That's probably the best bet."

"Pester is?"

Suddenly the odds board shifts again, but not, as he had predicted, in my favor.

"They're one in nine now," I say.

"It's just heavy betting," he explains. "It'll shift back. What's your name, pal?"

"Jim."

"I'm Chuck," he says, extending his sweaty hand. "Used to ride in the rodeo."

He's grinning, the eyes resemble coin slots.

"Up until I got injured. Then I went home, got married and got fat." He rubs a hand over his belly. "Too many hamburgers."

"Got a couple of horses now," Chuck says, as we wait in the sun for more beer. "No money in it really, but you have a good time. Where are you from?" he asks me.

"East."

"What do you do?"

"Nothing."

"Nothing?"

"Nope. I left it all behind."

"For what?"

"Don't know yet."

He stares at me for a moment in consternation, his mouth open. I indicate the odds board.

"It's going to shift again," he says.

We get our beers, and Chuck buys a hot dog. We walk down to the fence. With a minute to go, it has become shoulder to shoulder again, and a hush is beginning to spread among the crowd. The odds board shifts to three to two now. A little better.

"What would that pay?"

"Look at number three, my man. That's what I'd say bet on right now."

"But you told me number two."

He doesn't seem to have heard. "Jockeys in the irons," he says.

"And they're running," shouts a voice over the loudspeaker. At once, everyone is standing.

My horse finishes fourth. Chuck's smiling as people drop their tickets again. "Told you Pester," he says, spilling beer on my shoe. "Next race, just bet to show. And listen to me."

"Which?"

He looks up and down the program for several minutes, the substantial belly lifting and lowering, lifting and lowering.

"Gaelic Chant," he finally says and jabs me with the program. "Bet to show. Put ten bucks on it. Ten to show."

There are seven horses in this next race, and Gaelic Chant, from what I can tell, is the long shot. But I decide to put five dollars on him anyway.

"I know the trainer," Chuck says. "They've got a good team on it, my man. Good friend of mine, in fact."

We get another round of beers before the race, Chuck another hot dog, and stand in the same spot by the fence. The sun is beginning to drop through the grandstand, and shadows move across fields that seem suddenly still for a moment. The intoxication from spring breezes and Colorado Kool Aid brings strange thoughts. What if I were to take all of the money from the tackle box and bet it here this afternoon? It would be a way to hasten this journey.

In the fifth, Gaelic Chant finishes fourth. I take Chuck's measured advice in the sixth and lose again. In the seventh, I choose my own horse and win a dollar.

"You're too cautious," Chuck says, his back to me and his breathing raspy. "Now that you've gotten the feel for the track, you want to bet on a horse to win."

Having won a dollar, I feel some momentum at last and pick Streakin' Shasta for the eighth. But Chuck is shaking his disheveled hair. "Don't bet on that one, my man," he says, making marks in my program as I prepare to lay down twenty dollars.

He goes off for another beer and finds me just before post time. "What'd you bet on?"

"Shasta."

He winces.

"Shasta's the only horse that's Colorado bred in this race, pal, so that's going to be popular. I used to be in business with the owner. Years ago."

I check the program to see if there's any mention of where the horses were bred, but can't find any.

"You might be okay, though," he says.

The day's closing in a little now, and in the twilight shadows below the grandstand, I feel sunburn on my face. The edge changes as warmth seeps from the air; people's energies don't seem as frenzied. Gambling, even on Main Street, consumes people. A new American dream.

In the eighth race, Shasta hangs in the pack until the final turn, when he charges on the outside. Chuck is nodding already, another beer sloshing out of his cup, as if to say that once again he has made a correct prediction. But as Shasta comes into the straightaway, neck and neck with another horse, there's a collision. A jockey goes down and the crowd's collected sigh is so melodramatic it sounds rehearsed. My luck, I realize, as Shasta is led limping off the track, has not been good today.

We stand in the parking lot as the crowd files out. Chuck invites me to go up to the auction with him. "Get in," he says, indicating a rusty pickup truck with auto parts in the back.

The final light of the Colorado sun glows red on the tips of the barren bushes and the sprouts of new grass as we head west. A train moves alongside the highway for a while, then passes us. The sun is briefly bright along the barbed wire.

In Lamar, Chuck is disappointed to find that the auction is over. As an alternative, he offers to drive me to his house. "Just for a second. I need to check on my horses anyway." As he drives, the sky changes, and there's another kind of light, a cotton-candy color that evaporates on the brick houses.

His "house" is a trailer, a good ways off the highway, beside a field of winter wheat. A sorry-looking horse is grazing beside it. There's a crooked pink flamingo in front and two black children sitting on the broken concrete stoop. Chuck pats the boys on their heads and invites me in. It's messy. A black woman and a heavyset white woman are sitting at a Formica-top table, cans of Budweiser beside them. A black-and-white television plays without sound. The only light is the fading sun.

The women are playing cards, betting nickels.

"Hey," Chuck says, getting something from a kitchen drawer. "Where's Sammy?"

"He went with Robert," says the white woman. "Win anything?"

"Couple bucks."

"Couple?"

He goes in the back as I stand there looking at the women. We can all hear him urinating.

Chuck and his wife invite me to stay for dinner. As we sit outside around a picnic table at the end of the day, drinking Coors and eating hamburgers, I learn that Chuck and his wife are unemployed. They get by selling, trading and gambling.

Closing America Down

T he road takes me to La Junta, in Colorado's mountain country, where the Santa Fe Trail branched south and the most famous trading post in the West once stood. I search my old brochures from the fifties and sixties for an address or a phone number for the U.S. 50 Federation. "See It All On Highway 50." "Famous Fifty." "The Central Pleasure Route." "3,241 Miles of Pleasure and Relaxation." "America's All-Year Playground."

I dial the phone number listed from a ten-cent pay phone and am surprised to find that someone answers.

"Hello?"

"The Route 50 Federation?"

"Yes."

"The Federation still exists?"

"Well, yes. At least I'm still here."

The Federation, I find, is run these days out of Doyle Davidson's den, and its only function now is to publish a monthly newsletter. When I tell Davidson I've been traveling Highway 50 he insists I come over. After months of journeying on this road, I have found a Highway 50 guru.

For nine years—from 1961 to 1970—it was Davidson's full-time job to drive this highway, coast to coast, speaking to civic groups and lobbying for road improvements. There is no one, he says, who knows Highway 50 as well as he does. What happened to Highway 50, though, and what caused the Federation to shrivel up, is the thing that Davidson really wants to talk about.

"There was a story out there, a great story," he says as we sit in his study, "that people stopped listening to back in the sixties. You heard that story every time you drove across country on Highway 50. But almost overnight, it stopped."

Doyle Davidson, with some of the beer cans he collected while traveling Highway 50, La Junta, Colorado.

He's a tall man with a full head of white hair and an amicable smile that seems to appear at set intervals.

"Fifty was a great highway," he says, opening drawers and cabinets in the Federation "office" and handing me brochures. "We worked at it. We worked at making it the primary coast-to-coast route in the country. There were more historic sites and more national parks on 50 than any other road. And there still are. I'm still a great believer in Highway 50. It's a national treasure. But everything changed when the interstates came along. You can't fight the interstates, that's what it came down to."

As Davidson talks about the highway, his eyes take on a twinkle; an old dream is rekindled. Numerous times, without explanation, he stops talking so he can search through a box for the minutes of old Federation meetings.

He returns to why people stopped listening. "In the late sixties, the traffic counts dropped. All at once, everything changed. You could see it in the motels. There were so many motels closing down on Highway 50, and there weren't new ones opening. It was very sad."

"Was it the same on all the U.S. routes?"

"I think so. I think the whole country changed. The interstate got people places quickly. So most people took them. But it's about to change back again. That's what we're seeing. It's starting to change back."

He hands me several old newsletters to read as we talk. But before I have a chance to get through more than a sentence in any one of them, he's handing me something else. At one point, his demeanor turns grave, and he sounds as though he is reading a eulogy or describing a tragedy he once witnessed, which, perhaps, he is.

"The interstates closed down America for a lot of people. Suddenly, you didn't have to go through all these little towns to get where you were going, and people forgot they were out there. They stopped going to them. You stopped hearing about them. It really hurt this country. It closed it down."

Although interstates make up only 1.5 percent of the country's roads now, he tells me, they take 25 percent of its traffic. Davidson pauses long enough to get us a couple of Coors before telling me his theory—his dream—about how it's all going to change back again.

"People are starting to get interested in seeing the country again. There's no question about it. They're getting interested in American history all of a sudden. And the only way of seeing it is to get off those interstates."

I tell him it's a story I have heard often along this highway. In the hills of Ohio from Harley Warrick, on the Chesapeake Bay from Wade Murphy, in dozens of little towns that have refused to change. Progress doesn't work anymore.

Davidson's wife comes down several steps as we talk, ducks her head to see what we're doing, and goes back upstairs.

"For a while, there was all this emphasis on everything being new and modern in this country," Davidson says, "and I think things got moving too fast. It's only been in recent years that we've been thinking about preserving some of the older things. About preserving the environment. That's why you're starting to see more people out along Highway 50. Because it's a great and historic road, as great as any we have."

At the time Davidson was picked to travel Highway 50, he was working as president of the La Junta Chamber of Commerce. "They gave me two years to get it going," he remembers, "and I think we had eight hundred members by 1966." Davidson traveled more than sixty thousand miles a year on Highway 50 and gave hundreds of talks to Lions clubs, chambers of commerce and other groups.

"And you want to know what I've got to show for all that travel?" he asks, displaying a mischievous smile. He leads me outside, into the clear Colorado afternoon, to his garage, and undoes the padlock. Inside are rows and rows of beer bottles and beer cans, from floor to ceiling. More than three thousand of them, he says proudly, dating back to the mid-1860s.

"I began collecting them during my Route 50 travels," he says. "Whenever I'd find a beer I didn't have, I'd buy a six-pack and toss it in the back seat. Whenever I came back, I'd have to throw a big party to get rid of it all."

As Davidson hands over beer bottles—explaining where each came from—I see his wife again, looking at us from the back window for a moment.

The sun goes down, and he offers to show me around La Junta. The tour in his station wagon is quick. We stop at the Koshare Indian museum and then drive through downtown twice, running intersections as the stoplights turn red. What he really wants to do is drive with me along Highway 50 for a bit.

"So, you came all the way from the eastern end?" he says, leaving La Junta behind. "It's a great pilgrimage, let me tell you. You know, I was born on this highway. I was born and raised in Lamar. Then I was with the Chamber of Commerce in Delta, and that's on 50. And then the manager of the Cañon City Chamber, which is also on 50. Then I came to La Junta."

"I can see why you take such an interest in the highway."

"Oh, no," he says, and seems momentarily affronted. "It's not that. My interest in this highway is a very genuine one. There are more national monuments, more historic sites of great significance. ..."

He parks beside a field several miles outside of town, and we watch the traffic going east and west on Highway 50. We talk until after dark.

"It could go either way, I guess," he tells me. "It could get swallowed up, or it could get recognized as a great and historic highway. Like what happened in California. You know, 50 used to go all the way to San Francisco, and they took that away and made it Interstate 80. We fought that, but we couldn't beat it. One of these days I'm just afraid that's going to happen elsewhere, unless this other trend develops, which I hope it will."

The cars have their headlights on now, lighting up Doyle Davidson's face as he stares out at the road. "It's just up to which direction people are going to go."

Ute Country

N ear a little mountain town called Swink, a tractor-trailer truck carrying frozen chickens crosses the center line of Highway 50 and smashes a Subaru head-on. The car, which I am waved past, is barely recognizable, a crumpled piece of metal with a body inside. The image of this almost certain fatality stays with me for days as I drive the mountain roads.

I take the turns slowly and cautiously into Pueblo, where the first recorded explorers of Colorado stayed, Spanish officials searching for escaped Indian slaves in 1706. A hundred years later, Lieutenant Pike came to what is now Pueblo and built a three-sided log cabin. Pueblo was in Ute territory, but it was settled and named in 1842 by James Beckwourth, a mulatto trader who constructed an adobe fort that served as a trading post. He just decided—as people could back then—that the land was his.

As you travel west, a tattooed man outside of Pueblo tells me, you find that the land can't be ignored the way it can back east. It gets in the way. It makes people think differently, see limits.

The foothills of the Rocky Mountains come at night, affording passage to a region where Highway 50 winds in the paths of old Ute Indian trails. "The only Ute I have much respect for is Chief Ouray," Donald Rose, who works nights in a cafe near Pueblo, tells me. On his right arm, he shows me, is a tattoo that says Alberta. He met Alberta when he was in the Air Force, and as far as he's concerned she's dead now.

"I was told she died in a fire, but I never bothered to confirm it or not confirm it. Isn't that something, carrying somebody's name around for the rest of my life? Person who ain't even around anymore."

"What about Ouray?"

"Ouray was the peacemaker, man. Everything you see about the Indians around here, it has to do with Ouray.

"You can go up near Pikes Peak, man, the Utes lived up there. There's a place there called Garden of the Gods. It's like, seven hundred acres of mesa, studded mesa, red sandstone. That was the Utes' land. Get a buzz on and look at the Garden of the Gods. That's what the Utes were about, man."

"So what happened to them all?"

"They pushed them off on reservations. Never taught 'em nothing. After all they been through, they can't do nothing now but make blankets. But it was all their land, man. Whites decided they wanted it, and I guess whites wanted it more than the Indians. The homesteaders and mountain men came through here and they made the claims. The Utes never made claims. They moved around, like they owned the world."

The Choice

On the east side of Cañon City is the only Benedictine abbey in the state, a beautiful gothic monastery that is home to forty-five monks. On the west side, built into the sandstone mountains, is the Colorado State Penitentiary, the major industry of Cañon City.

I park the old Ford in the lot at the Holy Cross Abbey and have breakfast there at a table full of monks on a pleasant day in March. As I eat, I wonder, what makes someone devote his life to this sort of quest? Is it so different from what the rest of us are after?

Brother William tries to explain, as the other monks eat in silence. Now seventy years old, William came here when he was twenty-one and never left. He tells me about St. Benedict of Italy and the history of this abbey. But my curiosity is about his quest and his sacrifice.

"You have to understand," he says. "Everything we do is a form of prayer. It's hard for some people to comprehend that. Prayer is not just reciting prayers, as you probably do, huh? It is always being in touch. To be talking with God whenever you are alone; to be saying thank you for this beautiful day. That's what we strive for."

"Do you achieve it often?"

"No," he says, "not very often."

The temptation is to compare his life with mine, to wonder about the things he has missed by living in this abbey all his life. But he insists our quests are similar.

"You are out traveling, you say? Here we travel without going anywhere. We don't believe that being in a car and driving down the road for a year makes you any closer to God than being here and talking with him every day. You see, there are many different ways that people pray."

"Why confine your life to the abbey, though?" I ask. "Wouldn't you accomplish more by reaching out to people?"

Several of the monks clear their throats at this, but they wait for Brother William to answer. He slowly takes several sips of his soup, then sets his spoon in the bowl.

"Accomplish more? No. And, to put it in a nutshell, we do reach out. You can't love God unless you reach out. But there are many ways you can do this, huh? God needs to be brought to people in many ways, not just through preaching."

"So just by existing ..."

"Exactly, just by existing," he says, and I feel momentarily vindicated for my earlier question. "If I exist the way I should exist—don't get me wrong, I don't—but if I existed the way I should, then people would be moved to ask more, to see my life as an example. And in that sense, I am reaching out."

"Or would be."

He puts down his spoon and looks at me.

"Am I boring you?"

"No."

"Good."

After we finish, he shows me the grounds of the abbey and tells me the example of St. Benedict. "He started as a hermit. He thought that would be the way to go. He wanted to do it without the competition. You see, the existing forms of religious life were rather severe. The ones Benedict had experience with were sort of spiritual athletes, eh?" He pauses to laugh at his joke and then pulls a pipe out of his pocket. The breeze has a smell of fresh-cut lawn, the first cut of the year. "You see, they vied with one another to see who could fast the most or pray the most. St. Benedict said there were so many other people who wanted to do this but didn't fit in. So over a period of years, he came up with a more moderate idea, one that would cut out the competition."

"He was a rebel."

"Perhaps. The rebel with a cause, perhaps, yes."

Brother William soon turns the questions to me. He seems as curious about my quest as I am about his.

"What made you go out and do this?"

"I don't know."

"Well, make an educated guess."

"Suffocation."

"Aha. So it is a spiritual quest you are on?"

"In a way, I suppose."

He very slowly lights his pipe before continuing. "You see, perhaps that is what God has chosen for you. God chose this for me fifty years ago. He chooses a life for you and then you have the choice to accept it or not accept it. Some of those who don't accept it end up down the road, eh?" He means the penitentiary.

I want to know more about him and eventually succeed in turning the questions around again. Not having a family, not being with women, these things never bother him. What he regrets, he says, "is that I haven't done this as well as I could. I haven't lived it as intensely, as faithfully, as I could."

His eyes suddenly seem moist in the warm spring breeze, as we walk across the lawn toward the abbey building. "You see, asking people to give up something good serves a purpose. God tells people there's a certain order to things, but there are no absolutes. Our society absolutizes money and sex. He asked me to give them up, to show that you can do without."

He takes me into one of the dormitory rooms in the abbey where a very old man is sitting in front of a television. His hands grope in the air, as if he's trying to find us. He's blind. "He was one of my first teachers," Brother William says as he leads me downstairs into a dark corridor where there's a smell of mildew. He unlocks a door and lets me into a small room that is full of American Indian memorabilia. It is his hobby, collecting Indian artifacts: headdresses, jewelry, arrowheads and paintings.

"I'll show you what else I collect," he says and unlocks a second door. On the walls of this room are a dozen rifles. It seems a contradiction, a man devoting his life to God while collecting firearms. He smiles and sets down his pipe. "That's a very controversial thing nowadays, huh? No, it is not a contradiction. It is a hobby. If I used the guns to kill people, it would be a contradiction."

"Do you use the guns at all?"

"Occasionally. I hunt." There seems to be an edge to his voice.

"I met a student when I was in Europe, a Portuguese who lived in a colony in India where they believed you should not kill a mosquito. Eh? They had a profound respect for all forms of life.

They wouldn't step on an ant. Some religions say all life is sacred. Is that a different God?"

I accept this explanation, although I don't follow it. I begin to wonder what this has done for him, spending his life contemplating God. Has it cleansed him?

"I am able to pray to God, to be alone and appreciate the world. To thank God for this beautiful day. But I am still capable of evil."

"Evil?"

"Of course," he says.

My curiosity gets the better of me. "On what scale? Real evil?"

"Well, there was a person once who stole something from me. I found out about it, huh? I found out who it was, and, well, my reaction was not something that I liked. I think he's very lucky he wasn't there when I found out, because I felt such rage, such a hatred toward him for what he had done that I don't know what I would have done to him."

"You might have physically harmed him?"

"I don't know. I think maybe. It scared me that I could feel such rage after being here for fifty years."

He locks up this room with the guns, and we walk back outside, into the beautiful day.

I return to the abbey the next morning after watching the sun rise in Royal Gorge, where the world's tallest suspension bridge sways above the Arkansas River. One does not usually think about money in a place like Holy Cross Abbey; that's one of its charms. But in recent years, I learn, the story of the abbey has become one of finances. Unable to fund Holy Cross anymore, the monks have put the abbey up for sale.

"We have the problem of getting funding," Brother William says, reluctantly. "But we do not think it will be a permanent problem. God will take care of it. We've rented out some of our buildings, already, to a community college. The state rents out some of it. There is a police academy here also. So we get some money."

But the major problem, he says, is that people are no longer willing to come here to live and work for God.

"That is sad. The intense interest in learning to be a monk isn't there anymore," Brother William says.

"Why? What changed?"

"A good question. It started in the sixties, the spirit that was there in the sixties and the seventies, it had an effect on everybody. It made people take shortcuts, perhaps, eh?"

"Shortcuts?"

"Yes. It was very damaging."

"What kind of shortcuts? Spiritual shortcuts?"

"Yes, shortcuts through life. We are here as examples, to show that there aren't any shortcuts. There are only the long paths, the commitments. That's what we do here. We are an example, for people like you."

Angel on the Mountain

T he Arkansas River rushes through Colorado canyons in bright morning sunlight, its spray wispy in the winds that rise into the shade of pines and junipers. Occasionally, when there are gaps in the canyon walls, monoliths appear in the distance.

The old Ford's engine light comes on as the road passes Texas Creek, where cattle are grazing by the water. I stop just past a sign announcing "Cotopaxi," at a store called the Canyon Trading Post. A notice out front reads "No Bare Hunting."

As I open the screen door, a bear of a man, dressed in overalls and nothing else, comes out from the back. It is an ordeal for him. He seems to move partly forward and partly side to side.

"Any service stations nearby?" I ask, bringing groceries to the counter.

"Service stations?" he says, as though he's never heard of them. "Don't think so."

"Is this Cotopaxi?"

"Cotopaxi? Nope."

"I thought the sign said Cotopaxi?"

"Sign? Sign up the road? Didn't you see the little store?"

"The one that was closed?"

"That's right. Well, that's Cotopaxi. This here's West Cotopaxi."

Moving with difficulty, he puts my groceries in a bag and slides it across the counter. "You going west?"

I nod.

"Well, just a little ways past Salida, be looking for Shavano Peak. Stop when you get there and take a picture. This is the time of year when the angel comes out."

"The angel?"

"Yes, sir."

The legend of Shavano Peak is an old Indian story, I learn, which some of the natives still take seriously or say they do. A hundred years ago, the Ute Chief Shavano prayed at this mountain peak for a dying friend. Every April since then, when the snow melts in the mountains, the story goes, the angel becomes visible at certain times of the day.

"I'll be looking for it."

He winks. "Chew some gum," he says. "For your ears."

The road climbs the eastern slope of the Continental Divide, passing RV parks and whitewater rafting resorts. After Pancho Springs, there is suddenly snow on the ground as the highway crosses the eastern edge of the Cochetopa National Forest, a parkland full of old Indian trails where the afternoon light plays in the pine needles, on the firs and spruce and ponderosa pine.

When Shavano Peak comes into view, towering off to the right, I park and walk to the edge of the mountain slope. There's a fresh, bracing smell of pine and sage. Beyond Shavano Peak, dozens of other ranges, blue and purple and white, have come into view—the Sangre de Cristo, the San Juans, the Rubys.

At first there is no angel in the outlines of the rocks on Shavano, but I continue to stare, and before I leave I can see it perfectly—the wings spread upward into the clear blue sky. It's a reassuring message. The West is full of such symbols and signposts.

Beyond Shavano, the air turns to cool moisture—warm vapor clouds condensing in the cold winds—and small streams run through the hillsides. I stop again when we reach the Continental Divide to give the old Ford a rest and to take in the view. Icicles melt from the aspen. Nature, Emerson said, is fluid and ever changing. "To the attentive eye, each movement of the year has its own beauty, and in the same field it beholds, every hour, a picture which was never seen before and which shall never be seen again."

The Best Cook in Colorado

At the Cimarron Inn, an old wooden cafe beside the highway, the only customer is Ben Vigil, a dark man dressed in oversized pants, a plaid shirt and a bolo tie. He is seated at the lunch counter, hunched over a cup of coffee, when I come in. After a couple of sips, he surprises me by laughing loudly.

"The way you look to me," he says. "You thought I was a customer." He holds the smile. "No," he says. "Actually I am the owner." He speaks with a strong Spanish accent and a sense of pride at having fooled me.

I sit at the counter and order a Pepsi. The waitress, it turns out, is Ben's wife, Sally. "Yes, sir," he says, sitting sideways on his stool so that he's facing me. "Came here in 1953, with Lattermill Construction, to build that road. Later, I built the Blue Mesa Dam." Ben sips his coffee. It's a clean, old-fashioned place. On the walls, I notice, are pictures of children and several of John and Jacqueline Kennedy.

As I drink the Pepsi and then order another, I hear plenty more about Ben Vigil. He's from a Spanish-speaking community of New Mexico, and his ancestors were part Spanish, part Indian. He worked for everything he has, he tells me. "Education," he says, suddenly feigning modesty, "I don't have it. I only have grammar school education. But I am not afraid to tackle any man."

He is proud of his four children and of the tiny hamlet of Cimarron. When his wife comes back, he asks her to bring out "the book." "This will impress you," he says. He nods toward the entrance to the back room, which we both watch in anticipation.

Sally, a shy, polite woman, comes out with a paperback western and hands it to Ben, who hands it to me. It's called *Cimarron.* Ben is beaming as he passes the book over. "Go ahead," he says. "Borrow that if you like."

"It's about how this town used to be," Sally says softly.

Ben insists on driving me along Highway 50 to point out the part that he built when he was employed with Lattermill Construction. In the yard outside are dozens of junk cars, most of them wrecks, casualties of these precarious mountain roads.

"This is a brand new car," he says. The hood he taps is crunched up. "The people driving it were looking at a herd of elk up at the top of the hill here and"—he claps his hands together—"they went over."

The worst, though, was the accident that killed Abilene Maurer and her two little girls. Ben drives us to the top of a hill and asks me to get out and take a look with him. "See?" he says as if there's something to look at. "They saw this truck coming in her lane and she slammed on the brakes, but there was no shoulder on the road then. Nowhere for her to go. So the car went right under the trailer."

He turns into the wind and points, continuing to talk, although I can't hear any of it. When he faces me again, he's saying something about the chamber of commerce.

"We worked for the road improvements you see now. We were concerned because most of our children go over this same road in the school bus."

Back at the restaurant, Sally Vigil has prepared for us New Mexican–style enchiladas and *sapillara*. Ben gets two bottles of Coors, and we eat in the bar. There are no other customers all afternoon.

"New Mexican–style is not as spicy as the Mexican food you are used to," Sally says in a near whisper before leaving us alone.

"But better," Ben says, stuffing in his napkin. "She was the best cook in New Mexico," Ben says to me very seriously. "And now in Colorado."

The food is delicious, perhaps the best of this journey. As we eat, Ben runs a videotape for me on the television behind the bar. It is a tape of himself, receiving an honor called the Big Wheel Award, for his work promoting highway safety. His acceptance speech is as rousing as that of a seasoned politician.

"We need to work together," he says in the speech, "to set an example for the entire state of Colorado. We will make Montrose a beautiful city and Route 50 a beautiful highway all the way across America. President John F. Kennedy once said that we don't do this thing and that thing because it's easy. We do it because it's hard. We don't build the dam and these stores and the highway because it's easy. We build them because it's hard. So let us go ahead and lead this country to victory!"

Applause. It seems an odd speech, I think, to give when accepting a highway safety award. Ben gets up and rewinds, and he plays the tape over again. In the dim light of the bar, he waits, transfixed, until the speech ends a second time. He looks over occasionally to make certain I am watching. Then, he turns to me and elaborates.

"You see, it angers me when I hear people say that Americans are lazy or spoiled. If the American people are lazy, why are they paying the ranchers and farmers not to farm? How can we produce under those conditions? No wonder there's a problem with drugs, when people are not able to do anything. What we need is leadership, not salesmanship. We need a true leader. We need someone to back what that guy said."

He nods over his shoulder at a copper bust of JFK on the wall.

"'The entire world,' he said, 'watches to see what we shall do. We can't fail to try.' But America's failing, because we're always going where the big money is. We don't have the right leadership in this country, because a few Rock-a-fellers and a few Duponters can tell the president of the United States what to do. Only John F. Kennedy had the guts to stand against United Steel when they wanted to raise the price fourteen dollars a ton. I was working here at the time, and the guy from the steel company came through and he said to me, 'That son of a bitch, he ought to be shot.' And ninety days later, he was. Why did they shoot him?"

He's shaking his fork at me now.

"Because they couldn't buy him!"

Ben looks down at his shirt, where food has fallen. I'm finished, wishing there were more. He has not eaten even half of his dinner by the time Sally Vigil comes to take our plates. She blushes when I tell her how good it was. He goes on like this, offering simple answers to complicated problems, for much of the afternoon, drinking several more Coors and letting the bottles collect on the counter.

That night I lie in bed thinking about Cimarron, about the accidents and about the people who didn't make it through. On an impulse, I call back east, to my old life, surprised to find that things are still going on as they were when I left. The paper is still printing the news, and the people I knew are still doing the same things they always did. It makes me feel much closer to the old life than I imagined was possible.

After I hang up, I try unsuccessfully to read a few pages of *Cimarron*. It seems a mistake to have called.

Petroglyphs

I t rained during the night, and the fresh air smells of farmland. The road glistens; a rainbow traces the hills, arcing over
shining fields of drizzle. In the piñons and juniper trees, mist
steams, and occasionally small creatures appear—rock squirrels,
lizards, coyotes.

Up the road in Montrose—last known home of Ouray, the
great Ute chief—the highway is dry again and the air is warm. But
as the roadway nears Grand Junction, the early afternoon sky
turns black, and, for about three minutes, pieces of hail the size
of small tomatoes pummel the old Ford's shell. I bring her to a
halt in the middle of the highway and wait until it stops.

Then, winding down the Western Slope, toward Utah, the
highway is dry and hot again. Dirt and gravel roads lead off of this
lifeline, and, in the sunny afternoon, I decide to take one. A
crudely lettered sign instructs, "Petroglyphs 7 miles."

Petroglyphs are all that remain, in many cases, of the ancient
Indians who once roamed this land, and a seven-mile detour
seems worth the trouble to see some. But as the old Ford slowly
wobbles through this unmarked scrub desert, gravel yields to
dirt, and the dirt soon becomes studded with rocks. By the time
the odometer passes three miles, I am able to go no faster than
five miles per hour. I cross the narrow Gunnison River, and the
road becomes the width of a bike path. 4.2 miles. Oddly, there is
a house here and a man in the yard, who calls out to me.

"Not a traveling road," he shouts.

"I was trying to see the petroglyphs."

The man wipes a hand through his beard. He's wearing a tall
cowboy hat. "Not down here you're not."

The fading light of day is carried along in the short rapids of
the Gunnison. We stare at each other.

"Aren't the petroglyphs this way?"

"They're about eight miles down there."

"Eight miles? The sign—four miles back that way—said seven."

"Sign must be wrong then," he says, and I see that this detour is some sort of joke. "I'd say you could make it before morning, though. If you were to go by foot."

We both smile. This one's on me.

Nobody Ever Starved

E ventually, the mountains and monoliths that appear beyond the old Indian town of Grand Junction (formerly called Ute) win a kind of victory over the passive adventurer. For hours, for days, Highway 50 cuts through a country without cities, buildings or people. An illusion sets in that this land never ends. For the sake of sanity, I want to stop and get to know a town again, to make the country smaller.

I feel this way arriving at the little town of Green River, Utah. A shady place, quiet and green, with the sounds of lawn mowers and the smell of rhododendrons. The main road passes the Sleepy Hollow Motel, the Burger Drive-In, a Phillips 66 truck stop and the American Mexican Cafe before it narrows off into the unwelcoming desert.

At a diner on the main road through Green River, on a cool April afternoon, I figure my money on a sheet of paper. The news is surprising, but, strangely, not upsetting. There is only enough left for three or four weeks. At last, the journey has clear boundaries. Outside, above the glare of the empty road, a sign claims, "No Services Next 107 Miles."

I tell the waitress I've been traveling. Home address: Highway 50.

"Nice work if you can get it," one of the men says. Everyone chuckles. "Where are you going?"

"No specific destination."

"Might as well stay here, then."

"You want ice cream with that pie?" the waitress, a friendly matronly woman, asks when I order. "It'll be a quarter extry. Used to be, it come with it. But it's gotten so we have to charge a quarter extry."

I refrain from asking why "it's gotten" this way. Instead, I ask what kind of place Green River is for work.

"It's the best place in the world in a lot of ways," one of the men says. He's a well-tanned fellow who looks so similar to Anthony Quinn that I wonder, for a moment, if it's him. "If you're not too particular. Always something available.

"Used to be, we was considered the melon capital of the world. Best watermelons anywhere. Up until refrigerated cars. Then we lost the eastern market. Used to have three packing sheds here, and we'd ship 'em out by the truckload."

"They're still the best melons in the world, though," the waitress says.

"Sure," says another man. "Sweeter than most. But hardly too sweet. Just hit it right."

People in Green River love to talk about melons, I find, almost as much as they love to talk about the weather.

"Sun shines in Green River more than any other town in the nation. Did you know that?" Anthony Quinn asks.

"Why is that, I wonder?"

"Well, there's no reason for it. That's just the way it is. It's been proven. They could probably show it to you over at the library."

"How often does it rain?"

"Not much," he smiles. "Not very much at all. Some years, they say, it doesn't rain at all."

"None?"

"None at all."

"Best weather in the country," says the other man, who talks with his back to us. "That's really what we're famous for."

Green River is a town that seems too peaceful, too staid, to ever be disrupted by booms, but it's had several of them. The first was in 1882, four years after Green River was settled as a mail relay station and the year the Rio Grande Western Railroad came through. Early attempts to irrigate failed because of the unpredictability of the river. But eventually the flow worked and the melon market thrived.

Alma Scovill remembers when four or five passenger trains came through Green River every day and when everyone in town slept on their porches in summer because of the heat. Scovill, eighty, says he would help me find a job if I'm interested.

"That's the thing about Green River," he tells me. "The heat. Even at night. We have plenty of days when it stays eighty degrees

Alma Scovill and Shadow in the idyllic town of Green River, Utah.

all night long, and then all day too. Doesn't change more than a degree or two. Only place in the world like that. But that's why we grow the best watermelons right here."

That afternoon, Scovill and I sit on lawn chairs in the shade of his back yard, across the street from the library. The shadows of birds slide across the breezy grass and trees.

"I was a barber when I come down to Green River," he says. "Sixty years ago. I've done a little bit of everything since then."

Like most of the old people I meet in Green River, Scovill looks much younger than he is. I would have guessed sixty.

"Green River has a thing about keeping people young," he says. "It's a place that's always had something to offer. Back then, it was the trains. That's what brought me down. I used to stay up all night cutting hair. I come down here from the north. Road wasn't nothing but dirt back then. I remember it got awful dusty. Dust was rolling all over me. It took, I think, four and a half hours in that old Model T truck."

"How far?"

"Oh, sixty miles." He laughs.

"Been a lot of places since then, but this is where I knew I'd end up. Just something very peaceful about it. And another thing, nobody ever starved in Green River. You hear about people in other towns starving and being robbed. And, now, drugs. None of that's ever happened here in Green River."

"There must be drugs occasionally," I say.

"We get visitors who say that. They say exactly what you just said. But we haven't turned up any yet."

Scovill's dog, Shadow, comes sleepily out of the sunlight, sees me and turns around.

"I remember one time," Scovill says, not noticing, "this fellow broke his leg right about when your planting season got started, and the whole cockeyed town turned out and plowed his field for him.

"This house right here," he says, pointing at the old wooden-frame building next to his. "The owner was a war veteran and he had cancer. They had him up at the Vets' Hospital, and the one thing he'd been wanting to do was have his living room built out and a fireplace put in. While he was there, for six weeks, they had flood lights all over the place, and we had that fireplace built. He came home at three o'clock one night and they had a fire going for him, and he sat there all night looking at it.

"Finally, the next day, he went to bed and never got up. He died two or three days after that. The people of Green River furnished everything, he didn't pay a dime."

By my second day, I need no more sales talk about Green River. The quiet and the friendliness seem like a fairy tale. I visit Scovill again and ask about the melon business. Back in the thirties, when there was still a big New York melon market, he was a grower. "It's still something you can do, although it's a Utah and Colorado market now. Not national anymore."

I ask him how big Green River melons get.

"Well, minimum fifteen pounds. Get them as big as forty, fifty pounds sometimes. Of course, down in Alabama, I've seen them close to a hundred pounds. But they haven't got the flavor these ones have. I've eaten them all around the country and never found as good a flavor as these. It's not the size, it's the flavor."

I try to pin him down about the flavor.

"Well, they're real sweet," he says. "There's more sugar in them, I think. I don't know what the reason for it is, but I think it's the climate, that's a large part of it. I stake those vines some nights, and they'll grow that much further by morning." He indicates five or six inches, then extends the estimate to more like eight inches. "That's what it is. The night being as hot as the day."

These stories of magical melons and unworldly weather are intriguing. Although the people all seem to want me to stay, to like their town, I find that there really is no work. In fact, there is only one job available in Green River—part-time service station attendant. Still, it's a place that's hard to leave.

The First Gentile

One morning in the Green River library, Thelma Griffith Roberts, of Pocatello, Idaho, comes in. Roberts claims that she was the first gentile born in the town of Green River. She has stopped here today, with her son, to see if there are any records to prove it.

"Probably not true," she tells me. "Been saying it all my life, and now *he* says we have to prove it." It's her son, she explains, who feels that there is a need to provide proof.

"They don't have records as old as I am. Only thing I can tell you is I was born here on September the third, in 1907. I can't remember anything else, except my father sold race horses. I don't think there was even a race track; I think they just ran them off in the sagebrush back there." She looks out the window.

Thelma's family moved to Idaho when she was a girl, and she has spent the last sixty-six years in Pocatello, always thinking that someday she would return to Green River.

"I guess maybe I waited too long."

The library eventually confirms that there are no records showing that Thelma Griffith Roberts was the first gentile born in Green River. She blinks at the news and leans toward me.

"I guess as far as the world's concerned, I was never actually born," she says. "At least we'll never be able to prove it."

Before she leaves, Thelma Roberts tells me about Pocatello, where she worked as a housekeeper for seventeen years at the Brannock Hotel. "It's been torn down now, but they're making a park there. Every time I go by, I cry, because I worked there so long."

In the afternoon, I walk down the shady street that Alma Scovill says hasn't changed in forty years and then back to the main street cafe where the same people are seated with cups of coffee and slices of pie. Today I arrive at the right time, and they deal me in to their card game.

The Old Highway 50

ighway 50 and Interstate 70 are one and the same now through Utah, although the original path of 50 was north from Green River, toward Price and Salt Lake, and then west again, into Nevada. When I finally leave Green River, it is this earlier route that I take, into a lifeless land of mountains and monoliths. Mining country. The value of the land out here, miners say—sometimes with a strained optimism—changes with the world's technology. Copper, nearly worthless until 1880, became valuable with the invention of the electric light. Molybdenum had no worth until the production of steel alloys in the twenties.

The road, two lanes and bumpy, passes through a horse canyon in the late afternoon light, a sign that reads "Mine Road Closed" and then begins to climb again. Distant peaks block the sun. After another hour, Highway 50 arrives at the modest little town of Wellington, where Jim Norton's antler collection causes me to pull the old Ford to a stop. An arch of deer and elk antlers forms a gateway above Norton's driveway, and in the side yard, lined up for display, are hundreds more. Norton is there, trimming hedges.

"Feel free to take a look," he says. "Take as much time as you like. Be glad to answer any questions you have."

"What is this?" I ask.

"Family antler collection."

"Family?"

"The Norton family. These over here are ones I shot with a bow and arrow. These over here are ones I shot with a rifle."

He tells me story after story about where the antlers came from, and then moves on to dinosaur tracks and cattle skulls.

"The Indians used to come here and they'd want to buy the cattle heads from us. We finally found out that they were buying them from us and selling them at a profit, saying they'd been killed by the Indians.

"You know where they learned that kind of business, don't you?" Norton says.

I am spared the complete tour when a family in a loaded-down station wagon with New York license plates arrives and shows more curiosity than I do.

As some people collect coins or stamps or baseball cards, Jim Norton collects antlers. His side yard display—which is too unusual a sight for a traveler not to stop—is how he makes contact with the rest of the world. It is not, I decide, driving into the evening, such a bad idea.

"Feel free to come back anytime," he says, waving to me.

Up near Price, a woman dressed in faded jeans, a denim shirt and jean jacket is standing beside the highway holding a knapsack, miles from anywhere. When I stop, she stares at me in a strange, pouty sort of way but does not move toward the car.

"Out for a walk?" I say.

"Huh?" she says, not understanding.

"Strange place to be stranded."

"What?"

"I said it's a strange place to be stranded."

"Yeah?"

"Do you need a ride?"

"Depends. Where are you going?"

"Down to Highway 50. This is the old Highway 50 here. I'm following the old route, back to the current one."

"Huh?"

"I say I'm taking the long way around."

"What do you mean?"

"Nothing. It's not important," I say, but her frown is suddenly full of mistrust. She's young, a little chunky, with scraggly brown hair. Her face seems stained with dirt or tears. The wind picks up for several seconds, loud as an airplane through this empty red rock canyon.

"Who are you?" she asks, moving closer and giving the old Ford a looking over. "Where are you heading?"

"North, and then southwest to Route 50."

Jim Norton's antler collection, Wellington, Utah.

She stares at me, her mouth hanging open, but doesn't speak.

"What are you doing out here?"

She looks in the back seat, then asks me my name. She asks where I'm from and, again, where I'm going. There is a long scar on one side of her face and a Beatles button on her jacket.

Finally, she tosses her knapsack in the back seat.

"Okay," she says, getting in. "Just don't try anything."

She sits stiffly in the front seat for several miles, smoking one cigarette after another. The canyon walls turn dark and a coolness slips into the evening air.

"How long were you standing out there?"

She doesn't answer.

"You from Utah?"

"Huh?"

"Are you from Utah?"

"No."

"What's your name?"

"What difference does it make?"

"None."

"Sid."

"Excuse me? Sid?"

"Yeah."

Several miles later, she asks if I would mind her smoking a joint. I say no. Afterward, until we get to the tiny mountainside town of Helper, she doesn't say a word but laughs frequently.

In Helper, Sid says she feels like getting something to eat. The only place that's open is called Jimbo's Steak House. We stand inside for several minutes, waiting. In a back room, billiard balls clack and men swear. Finally, a large, bearded fellow wearing a black T-shirt comes out, carrying a cue stick.

"Help you?"

This strikes me as funny; the town is named Helper.

We both order beers, and Sid asks for a cheesesteak.

"You don't mind if I smoke, right?" she says to me as we sit at a table.

"No."

After the beer, she orders another. I've had only five or six sips of my first when she goes to the back room and asks the man if she can have a third.

"I'm sorry," she says to me, once it arrives, "if I seem a little uptight. But if you've, like, been through some of the stuff. It's like, you know, I'm like, I don't know." Then, louder, "It's like…"

I'm nodding.

"And it's not, like, I don't know. I guess, like, I'm catching a buzz now. But some people are just not, um, like, out for your best interest. You know what I mean?"

"Sure."

"And so that's the only reason."

"Sure. I'd be glad to listen if you want to tell me about it."

She looks at me suspiciously for a second and takes another swig.

"So, you know, I mean, like, okay. And this thing I was involved in wasn't working out, right? And I should have known that. But I'm just a little, like, okay, I'll try something else. Know what I'm saying?"

"Sure."

"But, it's like, okay, well, what do you do?"

"Me?"

"And it's, like, Dallas keeps popping up. You know. I'm not even sure why."

"Texas?"

"Yeah. And I'm like, you know. I don't know. It's just gotten weird, this Dallas thing. You know, it's like. I don't even know how to explain it."

She lights up another cigarette. In the back room, the men are talking loudly and crudely. Someone, in an astonishingly deep voice, says the word "fuck" repeatedly. There is no sign of life along the main street of Helper.

The cheesesteak seems burnt when the man in the black shirt brings it out. "There you go," he says, nodding nervously at Sid. "If you need anything else," he says to me, "don't be afraid to yell. I'll just be right there in the back." He walks with a slightly self-conscious gait back to the pool room. Shortly, the swearing resumes.

"I can't imagine what you would yell," Sid says, and it's our first and only shared smile.

Several times as she eats, Sid tries to explain herself, but each time it comes out as a garbled mess. We both end up looking out the window.

It's a long ride back down Route 10 to Highway 50 through the canyons. Most of the way, Sid snores and I stare at the lines in the road, trying to stay awake. A light rain comes out of the mountains as the road twists deeper into the night, causing halos to form around the streetlights. Sid is leaning against me as we go through Salina and on to Richfield, where, at last, I find a motel that is open.

Most of the people at this motel are sleeping with their doors open. Sid wakes up long enough to come in and take the other bed and immediately falls asleep again. All night, rain. I watch it through the opened door, slanting in the streetlight, and feel its cool mist. In the morning, there is steam on the shiny blacktop as I walk barefoot across the lot to turn in the room key.

Sid is still in the other bed, sleeping, when the phone rings to notify us that it is eleven o'clock. Check-out time. I shake her shoulders, and she reflexively shoves me away.

"Don't try anything," she says.

"Don't worry."

"What is it? Like, eleven o'clock? Oh, man."

Before leaving Richfield, I drop Sid off at the bus station. She wants to take a Greyhound to Dallas, she says. "It's just this thing that, like, came to me. I don't know what it's supposed to mean." She thanks me for everything, but it's as if she were thanking someone for passing her the salt. As the old Ford and I head west, it is with a sense of loss at not being able to connect.

No Markers

The map shows a Ute Indian reservation just south of the highway, in a place called Koosharem. But when I arrive in Koosharem, there's nothing but an old wooden diner in the spot where the reservation should be. The woman working there is the skinniest person I have ever seen, also one of the oldest. She holds a broom out as if for protection.

"I'm looking for the Koosharem Indian reservation," I announce. She looks out the window at the old Ford and then glares at me from across the room.

"It's not here."

"Where is it?"

"It's gone. They sold it."

"When?"

"Years ago. Ain't no Indians around here."

She watches as I get in my car.

Back up the road at the Grass Valley Mercantile Company and Post Office, a man who looks like Santa Claus out of uniform will not yield any doorway space as I try to enter.

"Excuse me," I say, squeezing through.

He watches closely as I purchase an orange and ask the young clerk about Native Americans.

"What do you want with Indians, anyway?" he asks as I leave, again making me squeeze past.

"I just wanted to see a reservation."

"What's to see?"

"That's what I wanted to find out."

"Don't see the need to. Be wasting your time."

There's no pretending otherwise: People in the West, some of them, anyhow, do not much like Native Americans.

"They got that controversy going now about the water rights

up north," the white-bearded man says.

"I've heard of it."

"They're putting it to the white man now, every chance they can."

"Hasn't the white man put it to them?"

He shakes his big head from side to side. "I ought to take you out to lunch and set you straight on a thing or two."

Instead, I drive back to Salina and stop at a little corner restaurant called Mom's. There's another reservation on the map, I see, near a town called Kanosh. I ask the waitress about it, and she looks away. "Never heard of it. What else'll you have?"

"Nothing else."

Four girls in a pickup drive by six times before I finish my lunch.

The road outside Salina is under repair. For miles, the old Ford can go no faster than ten miles per hour. After Delta, though, the highway all of a sudden becomes a freeway, and I take it down to Kanosh. Unlike the one at Koosharem, this reservation exists, although it more closely resembles a housing project. It consists of a clutter of rundown clapboard buildings, rusted-out cars and trash-strewn lawns out in the middle of an empty valley.

There seem to be no people here, until I come to the last house, where a short Indian man is scraping a deer hide and a woman is taking down laundry. They freeze in position as I pass by. And when I stop on the edge of the reservation, the man eventually comes over and asks if I want to buy something. Or if I'm just lost.

I tell him I'm traveling.

"With the government? Who with?"

"Nobody. Just traveling. Anything for sale?"

"We sell to Indian people."

"What do you sell?"

He points to the deer hide.

"You won't sell it to me?"

"Not this one."

Curious, the woman comes over too. She studies me closely, then, quietly, asks the man, "Who is he?"

"Don't know. He says he's been traveling."

The Pikyavit family, Kanosh, Utah.

"Where are you traveling?" she asks.

"Along Highway 50," I say.

"Well, you must've made a wrong turn somewhere." Both of them laugh at me.

"You going to make us stand here until we figure what it is you want?" she asks.

"Don't want anything. Just curious about the reservation."

The three of us look at the reservation, as if wondering why anyone would be curious about a place like this. The conversation thaws, and they invite me to sit down with them. Earl Pikyavit says that he might reconsider and sell me the hide if I'm really interested.

"How much?"

"Thirty dollars."

"Too low," his wife, Verna Pikyavit, says.

"Forty dollars."

This, it turns out, is how the Pikyavits—Ute and Shoshone Native Americans—get by. They eat deer and fish and sell deer hides and jewelry. They say they have all they need.

"We've always," Earl says, "lived the way we live now. I was born down there at the other end of the road."

"Tell him where."

"Under a tree." They laugh.

"We're not like the white people, see, who have to move around like flies all the time. The way you're doing. We've got everything we need right here," Verna says.

Spend enough time in one place, I think, and you lose perspective. Their clothes need washing; their yard is cluttered with trash. On the table is an old copy of the *National Enquirer*. Yet their eyes seem to come from a deeper place, far from these dirty surfaces.

"God gave us everything," Verna says. "We get by fine with what we've got."

"Nobody bothers us and we don't bother nobody else," Earl says. "That's fine with us."

At one time, the Kanosh reservation had eight thousand acres and was home to five hundred Utes. Now, there are only eighty acres and a handful of families, living in houses the government put up back in the sixties.

"What happened was they started taxing us," Earl says, as we sit out on frayed lawn chairs, and his voice tightens a little, "and they decided that they ought to take some of this land back while they were at it. Because all this land out here you see was Ute land. But the white man saw it was good land and they could use it for farming, so they sent some people down from Salt Lake to make up some reasons why they should take some of it back."

"But whose land was it?"

"Utes'."

"And they just took it?"

"See, back then, they didn't have no titles or nothing, so we didn't think that they could just come along and take what they wanted. But that's what they did. We weren't educated to know about those things. Land just closed in on us. Now, we look at it and we know it's not ours."

Verna is more upbeat. "We're able to find things like they were before the white people came along without any trouble. The white man don't bother us. We don't dislike the white people. We just believe in staying with other Indian people."

I ask Earl if he feels the same way, and he stares back at me. I seem, for a moment, like an invader, an intruder in their world.

"I'll put it this way," he says. "We're not educated, but we've taught ourselves things. We're educated in our own ways. We know how to get by on the land, which is an important thing that most people can't do."

Earl's and Verna's black hair is whipping over their faces as the afternoon light turns. My curiosity wins out again. I ask if they ever have dreams of getting out, of trading their lives for different ones.

"I guess there are a lot of things you'd like to be doing," Earl says, "but you accept that you aren't going to be able to. There's a lot of things you'd like to be doing, but you don't know how."

The look in his eyes, after he says this, is perhaps the saddest moment of the journey. I don't forget it. For weeks it stays on my mind.

For the children at Kanosh, it's different. They've gone to school, and many are moving off the reservation. But Earl and Verna Pikyavit plan to stay here. Earl stands up slowly before I leave and shows me the little cemetery behind his house.

"That's where all my relatives are buried," he says, "and that's where I'm going to be buried."

Most of the graves, he says, are unmarked or are marked by just a stone. "That's how they used to bury them," he says. "That's where I'm going to end up. That much I'm sure of."

They wave as I start up the old Ford and head back down the long road to Main Street.

Running Low

After Green River and Kanosh, I feel a strange isolation. I sense it as I walk up and down Main Street in Delta, Utah, and feel conspicuous. Out of sync with those who stay put.

Trying to conserve money, I sleep in the old Ford for several nights on the outskirts of town and wander Delta, a small farming community, during the day. On the corner at Service Drugs, the postcard rack reflects the alien nature of this land. There are giant animal postcards—a seven-foot rabbit and men carrying a rack with a gigantic grasshopper. Things are bigger here in Utah, a blurb says. I ask Ward Killpack, who has owned Service Drugs since 1950, what it means.

"Nothing," he says. "Although, occasionally, people'll come through and ask me where they can see the seven-foot rabbits."

"What do you say?"

"I give them very clear directions. Send them way out into the desert. One time, a family come all the way from California. Said they'd heard about the seven-foot rabbits of Utah. I'll tell you something, though. Those same pictures are used on postcards in Nevada."

My first time in Pop's City Cafe on Main Street, I ask the waitress about sweet milk. The beverage list includes sweet milk for fifty cents.

"Sweet milk?" she says. "Oh, that's just regular milk."

"Why's it called sweet milk, then?"

"No reason, really."

"Okay. Sweet milk, scrambled eggs."

She writes it down, taking far longer than I would expect anyone to take with such a small order.

In the evenings, men gather here for slices of pie and cups of coffee and look up each time a car passes. They nod to me and say hello. The conversations, mostly, are about the mines. The men who come in for pie and coffee are miners, I discover.

"Ever hear of beryllium?" one of them asks one evening, trying to feel me out.

"Sure," I say.

"Well, the largest deposit in the world of beryllium, she's sixty miles. Out there."

He turns and points toward the bathrooms.

"What's beryllium used for?"

"Well, she's got one main use, and that's on the hulls of rockets."

"Most of the mines aren't going so good, though," the man next to him says. "Silver's not worth much at the moment. Guess gold's going all right, and so's your copper."

"They say she's copper up near Ely."

"I haven't heard that. She's gold out near Austin, Eureka. Would you say?"

"I'm only hearing it."

Delta is peaceful, a little like Green River, but there is something different here. It is almost not surprising when, one evening, several men stand in a semicircle around me, as I eat a piece of blueberry pie with a glass of sweet milk, and demand to know what it is I want.

"You need work?" one says, his chest thrust out, thumbs in his pockets.

"Not really."

"Well, what do you need?"

"I don't know," I say. "Do I look like I need something?"

"They say you're sleeping in your car. People who sleep in their cars need something. We'd prefer you go somewhere else. We'd prefer not to have you arrested."

So I leave Delta, Utah, and head west. But I do not want to reach another town just now. I want to wander, out onto these cracked alkali flats, among the seep weed and salt bush and greasewood. It's Saturday night, oldies night across America, as I enter the desert. The sounds of Chuck Berry and Del Shannon reach the old Ford out in the wild, windswept sink where the only signs of life are lizards and coyotes.

When People Came Out

A fter the desert, I find a nice room in Ely, Nevada, and take a long shower.

On the fronts of hotels along the old brick main street, neon blinks. At a corner is the Nevada Club, which never closes. Slot handles crank. Half a block down is the old Ely Hotel, famous for its Basque cooking. In the lounge I order a beer from Marianna Goyhenetche, who owns the place.

"Quite a few people in town tonight," I say as she serves up.

"Not many."

"Seems like."

"Not so many," she shakes her head and goes off to the dining room. A dozen people are seated there at a long table. I hear her say, "You boys okay? Or you need something else?"

"We're fine," one of them says.

She comes back in and wipes off the counter, for something to do. She's a small, energetic, white-haired lady.

Ely is a mining town, but right now, she tells me, the mines aren't going. The prices are down and the people aren't here. Ely used to be a Basque town, she says, but the Basques are gone as well.

"The Basque immigrants came a hundred years ago to become miners. Just like the Chinese did."

There are only three Basque families left in Ely, but Marianna, who is French Basque, feels an obligation to carry on the tradition.

"I could have gone off and done something else, but you don't do that. That's the way traditions die." She points out the window. "Right there across the street," she says. "That's where I was born."

Marianna's friend, Bob Perry, comes in, sets his hat on the bar and pulls up a stool. He's a tall, silver-haired, senatorial-

Marianna Goyhenetche behind the bar at the Ely Hotel, which she owns in Ely, Nevada.

looking man. In the back, I hear Marianna say, "You boys want me to get you anything else, or do you want me to come back? You sure you have everything you want now?"

"This bar," Bob says, pointing at me. "Used to be lined with people right up to the wall here. And it was open twenty-four hours. Only time you got to clean the damn thing was on Sundays when the people decided to go to church on the hill."

"What changed it? The mines?"

The suggestion takes him by surprise.

"Not the mines," he says. "Television."

"Television?"

"Yes. This was before you had television. In those days, people'd come out on the street at night and talk to one another. Nowadays, people don't even know how to have a conversation because of television. And some of the time, when they do want to socialize, it turns out that what they really want is to go over to somebody else's house and watch the television."

Marianna comes back and puts her elbows on the bar, facing Bob but talking to me.

"He's right," she says. "Television is what changed this town as much as anything else."

"It was much more exciting back in those days, before television."

"Even if there weren't more people in Ely," Marianna says, "there were more people who came out."

The "boys" from the back room—six middle-aged men, five of them bald—go out, and Marianna comes from around the bar to pat them all on the back and thank them.

There's a ten o'clock curfew for minors in Ely, but it isn't strictly enforced. Sometimes the children of prostitutes wait on the streets for their mothers to get off work, or they go in the bars or the casinos. Prostitution is legal in this part of Nevada.

If there's trouble in Ely, it comes mostly from the visitors, Jim Ramsey, manager of the Ely Hotel, tells me. "That's because most everyone here is a long distance from where they came."

I order another beer, but Ramsey tells me to try a Picon Punch instead. It's what the hotel is famous for.

"It's a blend of five different drinks."

"The punch hits you later," Marianna says. She has finished saying good-bye to the "boys" and returned to the bar.

"We've had some incidents here," she says, as Ramsey fixes the drink. "Like, once, we had five guys who shot each other. All gay. The door still stands with the bullet holes in it."

Jim sets my Picon Punch on the counter. "Drink it slow at first."

"Don't worry," I say, after the initial sip.

"They stayed at my hotel. Top the stairs, first door. They shot at each other."

"Fatal?"

"It became fatal. They went up to Murray Canyon, took Highway 6 up to the top of the mountain, and they shot one another. Only one of the five survived, I think."

"Was it just one?" Ramsey asks.

"I think so."

I wait for her to tell more. But that, evidently, is all.

"What was it about?" I say.

"Nothing. They were goofed up, that's all. When you're goofed up, you're goofed up."

I drink the Picon Punch and watch the cars go by outside, feeling a little bit goofed up myself. Bob Perry stands in the doorway for a while, and Marianna goes back to the dining room.

"The main thing wrong with Ely now," he says, "other than television, is too many parking lots. All these parking lots; they used to be buildings here."

"A lot of old hotels burned down," Jim Ramsey says.

"Most all of them did. Nothing but parking lots now."

I finish the Picon Punch and walk out into the Nevada night toward the bright neon of the Nevada Club, which is, clearly, the main hangout in Ely. Inside, a man in a sequined jacket is on stage, singing "House of the Rising Sun," backed by a brassy band. I play the nickel slots for a while. A bleached blond comes over after a few minutes and watches, smelling strongly of Giorgio.

"Buy me a drink?" she says after a while.

"All right."

I order a sloe gin fizz for her and another beer for myself.

"So what do you do?" she says, turning sideways, her nylons making a sandpaper sound.

"Nothing," I say.

"Sounds like fun."

"It has its high points."

She looks me over with a disingenuous leer.

"You don't do anything?"

"Travel."

"That's all?"

"I traded my life in a year ago."

"For what?"

"It isn't clear yet."

"Uh-huh."

This has temporarily derailed her, but she tries not to let on. She has a beautiful, plump, girlish face but has covered it in too much makeup.

The singer goes into a raucous version of "Proud Mary," and it becomes difficult to hear each other. Several times I look over and she's staring at me. I stare back. It's like being in high school again. She asks more about the journey, its lack of purpose, and for some reason it begins to genuinely interest her. The way she looks at me, I can tell there is no sense of awe but, perhaps faintly, of recognition; she has done something similar and is wondering why people do things like this. The anticipation of a heroic quest turns into a blur of motion.

She drives us to her apartment and invites me in for a drink. It is a tiny, one-room place but nicely decorated. Her name is Ginger. We talk and listen to jazz and drink. Finally, as the sky turns light outside her curtains and the sound of birds fills the air, she offers herself to me for thirty dollars.

In the mountains the next morning, a train called "The Ghost Express" takes tourists to the sites of old mining camps. Ely began in the 1860s as a gold mining camp. In 1869, a lead blast furnace was built here and a mill to store deposits from the gold mines. The town is named for John Ely, who bought a mine for thirty-five hundred dollars and later sold it for almost half a million. During the heyday of Kendicott copper, there were ten thousand people living in Ely. Some of their shacks are still visible on the hillsides outside of town.

Leaving Ely, I pass a sign that reads "U.S. 50, The Loneliest Road in America."

Highway sign in central Nevada, proclaiming U.S. 50 "The Loneliest Road in America."

Fixing Old Things

I meet Carol Bleus at the bottom of a long, gently sloping hill in Eureka, Nevada, a town where the crossroads are called Silver Street, Gold Street and Mineral Street, and where none of the houses has a number. The mailman just knows where everybody lives.

"What is that?" I ask, indicating what looks like an old gothic church beside the hillside.

"My house," she says.

It seems too old, too precious, to actually be someone's home. She smiles. A small, gracious woman.

"It used to be a church, and bit by bit, my husband restored it, made it into a house. He's in Ely today, restoring an old whorehouse."

"Oh? What do you do with a restored whorehouse?" I wonder.

"He's going to turn it into a bed and breakfast. That's what we do, we fix old things."

They came to Eureka, she says, from California because they wanted to get away from the crowds.

"We saw this pile of rocks and Frank said, 'What I could do with this. ...'

"So we bought it for five thousand dollars. That's what we do now, fix things. Do you want to come in?"

"Sure."

"Get out of the wind."

I follow her through a room with beautiful Chinese chairs that came out of the underground tunnels that once connected the town's businesses, up a wooden spiral staircase to a half loft. We sit in the kitchen and she offers me a beer. This day is funny for her, she says, because it's the first time she's been away from her husband since they were married. She brings the beer and sits next to me at the table.

"You know, we stayed right here while he was working on the house. And we've never been separated since. The creek was running that year, so I did the dishes in the creek. There was no plumbing or water. We had to use the bathroom facilities up at the park.

"It seemed like it used to rain every day that first year. Every afternoon, we used to have thunderstorms. You'd get flash floods and it would just come in the front door. I don't know how many times we'd wake up and there'd be two feet of water on the floor."

"Did you ever want to just pack it in?"

"We didn't have any money. We cut our bridges and we couldn't go back. We'd work and spend the money we had, and we'd stop and then work again for a while. Do some kitchens for people in town. Little by little by little. That's how things get done."

She describes the house as an evolving piece of art that Frank will work on for the rest of his life.

"It's like what you do with your life, I guess. You just gradually keep working at it. Making it better."

The sun has begun to go down along the leafy, windy hillside when we hear Frank limping up the stairs. I sit up straight. Her husband, she whispers to me, suffered a brain aneurysm several years ago and is partially paralyzed.

When he enters the kitchen, Frank Bleus frowns at me and then at the beer bottle. He gets a beer from the refrigerator and sits next to me. He stares for a while.

"Dear, I've just been talking with this man about the house."

"You're from Maryland?"

"Yes."

"Where are you headed?"

"West."

He sips and stares a little more.

"Miner?"

"No. Just traveling."

He sets the bottle down, and it makes a fresh ring on the wood, then he limps over toward the window and looks outside at dusk coming on.

Last Frontier

Until it reaches Fallon, Highway 50 cuts through what Nevada natives like to call Real Nevada. In Real Nevada, the range is still open, the air is pure and the cattle graze right out on the highway. During windstorms, the sky can become so choked with dust that the only thing a traveler can do is park his car on the highway and wait until it stops.

"The governor don't even visit this part of Nevada," a cattle rancher with a gas station in the Diamond Valley says, squinting at me in the purple light of sunset. I'm filling the old Ford with gas and squinting back at him. "You tell me the last time he's been to Eureka."

"I can't."

"Well, no. That's because the governor's never been to Eureka. He's scared of this part of the state."

"Scared?"

"Sure."

I hand him money for the gas. The alkali flats have turned pink in the distance.

"The places that control Nevada are a few cities in the West. Vegas. Reno. Carson. That's Nevada for a lot of people. But that ain't Real Nevada. We call it an extension of California." He winks at me.

Dwight Eisenhower, I learn, took this same route through Real Nevada back in 1919 with the U.S. Army's first transcontinental convoy team. Somewhere around here, sand drifts covered the road, and the convoy became stranded. It was the experience of being stuck in Real Nevada that prompted him, many years later, to push for a national interstate system.

The towns in Real Nevada have turn-of-the-century main streets and populations of just a few hundred. As I pull into Austin, there's a sound of accordion music in the night air. Lee

Cooley, the town's only live entertainment, is playing jubilantly at one end of the bar for a crowd of about a dozen at the Golden Club. Lana Bare, the bartender, is leading them all through a sing-along of "On Top of Old Smokey" as I come in. A huge Indian man is singing louder than everyone but always a beat behind. I stand next to him and sway slightly.

When the song ends, I order a beer and face the open doors.

"Your first time in Austin?" Lana asks. She says it as if she's asking about my virginity.

"Can you tell?"

"You just seem a little, I don't know, bewildered."

"I guess so. I didn't know there were still towns that looked like this."

"Same reaction everyone has the first time."

The accordionist, I see, is wobbling as he tries to stand up. He grabs onto the huge Indian man for support, but slams into the bar anyway. "I'm drunk," he explains as he passes us on his way to the bathroom.

"He's already played two other saloons tonight," Lana says. "He didn't want to come here, but I went down and picked him up. It's Saturday night. We needed music."

Besides being the only live entertainment in Austin, she says, Lee Cooley is the only mechanic. When he comes back from the bathroom, I tell him about the old Ford and the journey we have been on. He requests a look.

"Strange engine," he says, after I lift the hood. "Homemade?"

"More or less."

He nods. He seems as clear and alert as anyone.

"Best engines I've ever seen are homemade. Can't make much sense out of them sometimes, but they run better than any engine that comes out of a factory. I like an old car with a homemade engine. They just have a lot more personality than one you get off the showroom."

At last, someone who understands the old Ford.

Back inside, Lana is starting a sing-along of "Streets of Laredo."

"That's my cue," Lee Cooley says. He takes up his accordian again and begins to play as the wind gusts loudly up Main Street, Austin, Nevada.

The golden light of dawn burns moisture from the cracked earth. The morning desert sky is a cloudless blue. To the left are long dried-up lake beds where the trains never stopped. Over New Pass, the low sky shimmers. Nearby are the ruins of an overland mail station.

By the time I get to Middlegate, the old Ford is overheating, so I stop to let her drink. Middlegate, just off Highway 50, past the junction with state Route 2, has only three businesses and a population of fourteen.

"It used to be fifteen," Fredda Freeman, who runs a bar and restaurant here, tells me, "but one fellow died from a heart attack."

Freeman moved here, she says, because she figured no one would ever be able to bother her in a place as isolated as Middlegate. She came from Austin eleven years ago.

"Solitude," she says, as I sip on an orange juice with ice. "It really seemed to me like the last frontier. I raise my own pigs, raise my own chickens. I love the area."

I wonder, sitting there listening to her, if this is what I've really been after on this long and soon-to-be-ended journey, a place where I am left alone. The wind kicks up outside, rattling windows and filling the air with dirt. I begin trying to figure whether or not I have enough money to make it to the coast.

"So what's wrong with your car?"

"Pardon?"

"Your car." She points. "What's wrong with it?"

"Just needs a rest. Does it ever get lonely being out in the middle of nowhere like this?"

"Heck, no. I cherish this place."

But even the most isolated areas—secluded places like Middlegate—are vulnerable to a world that still believes in change. For the past five years, a sonic test range has been located just miles away, and Middlegate can't pretend that it's not there. One recent afternoon, Freeman was standing in the bar and Navy planes flew so close that all the windows in the building shattered.

"They'd probably like to force us out eventually," she says. "Last place in the world I figured anybody'd ever be able to bother us, but that's what they're doing. There's only fourteen of us; I guess they figure we're not so important. I got home one day and they'd blown out all our windows there too, and knocked the trailer off the blocks."

"Aren't there any kind of reparations?"

"All they say is, 'Gosh, we're sorry.' See, they make you do all the legwork. Fill out papers, make long-distance calls and then, finally, the very last thing they'll do is send out an investigator and say, okay, we can cover you for the damages."

"How often does it happen?"

"Every six months now. They make us feel like we're not supposed to be here and there's nothing we can do about it."

Deeper into the emptiness of Real Nevada is Dixie Valley, where the late afternoon sky seems to shake with the sounds of airplanes. Turk Tschettar is the only resident left in Dixie Valley, and he says he has no plans to leave.

"I like the emptiness out here," he tells me, standing on the porch of the ranch house he has owned for twenty years. "Before the Navy decided to turn it into a test area, it was kind of my retreat. Used to have six or eight neighbors. Now I'm the only one left here."

Tschettar was born in Michigan and lived for years in the Nevada capital of Carson City, working for the government.

"I just decided I didn't want to be around the hustle and bustle anymore. I wanted to live out where it's just me and the earth and the sky. Just the basics."

Dixie Valley is owned by the Navy now, and the government wants Tschettar to move.

"If you live in a place long enough, it's your home and no place else feels right. This is my home. I'm not going to move from it."

He stands there on the porch, looking out over his valley. The only sounds are the wind and the planes, and sometimes it's difficult to tell which is which. In these vast open spaces, without boundaries, without stops and starts, anything seems possible, even one man standing alone against progress.

The Oasis

Two lanes of highway trace the eastern front of the Sand Springs Mountains, then climb a pass between the Stillwater and Sand Springs ranges before Sand Mountain, a sixty-foot-tall, two-mile-long sand dune in the desert. Then, there's Fallon, a neon mirage in the shimmering salt flats. It's a commercial and farming center with huge casinos and chain motels marking what must be the end of Real Nevada.

At a restaurant called the Waterhole, I order lunch and talk with the waitress about how Fallon has changed over the years. Through a misunderstanding that I'm unable to correct, she thinks I'm inquiring about buying property.

"Here," she says, bringing me a beer and a copy of a local paper called the *Big Nickel.* "I don't know what price range you're looking at but this'll give you some idea."

She sits down next to me, half on the seat, half off, a giant of a woman with a surprisingly gentle voice. Outside, the sky has darkened around the brightening casino lights. Cars go up and down Maine Avenue.

"Here you go," she says, circling one. "Thirty-five acres, by the railroad."

"What's the advantage of being by the railroad?" I wonder.

"You know," she says, shrugging evasively, "that's just personal preference. Now, here you go."

She circles two more and abruptly stands. "Hold on."

I look at what she has marked.

"Near Rye Patch Reservoir: six acres between freeway and Fox Hole Tavern, $9,000; financed, $2,000 down."

"Forty acres, fifteen minutes to Reno. View, power, prices $30,000 to $39,000, nothing down, no qualifying."

Good deals, if Nevada was where I wanted to wind up. But I

sense the journey concluding and decide to make it coincide with the end of the highway.

Outside of town, a tractor is cutting a slug trail in the dirt where alfalfa is left to dry. Things are growing again. It's haying season. I drive back into the desert, considering what I will do once the money is gone and the highway has run out. As I think about it, the road suddenly turns to dirt and follows a barbed-wire fence toward a glow that looks like a campfire. I realize that, not paying attention, I have drifted off of Route 50. Ahead, through the smoke, are truck lights and a herd of cattle.

"Can't go further up this road," one of the men by the campfire says, stopping me. Another one stands in front of the car so I won't make a run for it. "They're moving cattle up there."

The three of us stare at the cattle moving, loud but distant, through darkness, toward the lights of the ranch houses. Piñon wood cracks in flames; the smoke rises. There are still warm shades of blue in the sky.

"I guess I did get lost."

"This here's all private property."

"Hard to tell where the private property begins," I say. "It's not marked."

The men don't say anything. They watch me as I cross back over the invisible barrier that marks where the private property ends.

In Stagecoach, the streets are all named for western trails. There's Cheyenne Road, Cochese Trail, Cimarron Trail and Santa Fe Trail. Ahead, the mountains are snow covered. I stop in Dayton, where the first quartz mill in the state was built and where, on a corner, is the Corner Bar. I go in to pull the slot handles, then move on, past the Moonlight Ranch, one of the state's best-known whorehouses, to Carson City, the capital of Nevada.

Shortly after getting a room at the Highway 50 Motel, I decide to bet half of what I have left in the Golden Nugget casino. I lose it at the blackjack tables within three hours and realize that this journey is all but over.

Wedding Ship

There is an old idea—a simple, sentimental notion—that becomes the guiding thought as I head toward California: You don't realize what things are worth until later. As my money goes, the mundane and routine attains a new value. The highway crosses Eagle Valley, toward the Sierras, and for the first time in months, the old life begins calling again.

Highway 50 ascends Clear Creek Grade, where the canyon walls and slopes are wooded with pine and fir, mountain sage and the occasional bright red colors of snow plants. The old Ford makes a rude rattling sound that seems to offend the other traffic here. Drivers scowl as they pass us in the Yayabe Forest, where there are cool, beautiful views through the tall pole pines. Soon, there is snow on the trees.

At a summit, elevation seven thousand feet, and through the V-shapes of the pines, there's suddenly a view of Lake Tahoe sparkling in the afternoon sunlight.

The road winds through Glenbrook, an old lumber town, where I stop and sit on a rock cliff high above the lake, just listening to the back and forth of the water, the pines creaking slightly in the windless cool air. Still: one highway, as if all this I have passed through is in some way "united."

When the first explorers came west, they did not know that there was another range of mountains after the Rockies. The Sierras were a surprise. In 1850, Lake Tahoe did not even appear on maps. But the discovery of Nevada silver deposits in 1859 made travel over the mountains essential, and the narrow Indian trail that wound by the lake—now Highway 50—suddenly became congested. Way stations and inns were erected, the road was widened, bridges were built and tolls were charged.

I park again and eat lunch, sitting on the old Ford's hood, not far from where a man is fishing. A little girl is in his truck, reading a comic book.

"How do you like that?" he says, tilting the bucket to show me a large mackinaw trout. The air is crisp and the water clear.

"Good size," I say. He nods proudly, a sturdy, muscular man, friendly.

"Probably six pounds, maybe a little more."

The rocks slope down to the lake and you can see some of them through the water, its surface rough, but it's not windy enough for whitecaps. Across the lake the sun comes through the clouds, and there's a patch of light on the water; beyond it are snow-covered mountains. Then the clouds open, and you can hear the steady sound on the rocks.

"Beautiful land here."

He doesn't answer right away.

"You just wish people'd leave it alone," he says at last. "If you'd seen this place fifteen years ago."

"Yeah?"

"They got a problem now with the conifers dying. It's mostly caused by the use of salt in the wintertime to melt the snow. It used to be they just shut the whole lake down in winter. The evergreens, the red fir, Douglas pines, they're all turning brown on the highway side, the bristles are falling off. Especially up by the state line. It's dying, but you can barely see it."

He lets me watch the fishing line for a while as he goes to the bathroom. The little girl opens the door of the truck, sets her comic book down and comes over. "You want me to hold it?" she says, taking it from me. "I'll hold it." We watch the float out over the indigo waters. The lake is clear enough that we can see silver trout moving in it, but there's no way to coax them to the hook. "They're just playing right now," the girl explains.

As a final luxury on this journey, I decide to stay nearby at Zephyr Cove, a collection of rustic lakefront cabins among the pines: redwood-stained wooden buildings with green trim around the windows, roof lines and doors. The path to the outdoor bar is strewn with pine cones, and I go down this first night, have a bourbon and watch the *Dixie* getting ready for her 7:30 dinner cruise. The lake surface ripples and darkens as a wedding party walks down the long dock and boards the boat. I drink slowly, thinking about the ritual of the wedding.

Back in the cabin, the fire feels warm on my face. There's a sense here of wanting the sun to go away slowly, to enjoy it for as long as possible. I stay in Tahoe for several days, just sitting in the cabin or on the porch and hiking alongside the lake, trying to come to some epiphany. I don't.

In the mornings, if you stop thinking, you can hear the lake water again. In the evenings, at 7:30, there's another wedding party coming down the dock.

The Land of Stories

Ighway 50 winds alongside the American River back down to flatlands, following a route that was once nicknamed the Silver Trail, a fortune seeker's road. Like the Northwestern Turnpike over the Alleghenies, the Silver Trail provided a link to the rest of the continent. It helped the nation pursue its grandiose goal of unity.

After many months of traveling this highway, I come to the state whose motto is "Eureka" (I have found it) with a sense of resignation rather than exhilaration. Running out of money and highway is like waking from a vivid dream; there is no returning to it. Just outside of Sacramento, without notice, Highway 50 widens and disappears into the Interstate, and the journey becomes a chimera. There is no sign here telling travelers the distance back or indicating that there is an eastern end to this centralmost of the U.S. routes.

I follow huge green Interstate signs to the California coast, to the spot where Highway 50 used to go, past the blurs of suburban neighborhoods, as the gas needle on the old Ford drops toward empty. On the docks where the country ends, I watch darkening bay waters in the fog. I will return east, to what I left, owning nothing, perhaps, but bringing back something of incalculable worth: Main Street wisdom. What we ultimately become, after all, is determined by stories, by what we hear, by what we tell others and by what we tell ourselves.

In the quiet of the western edge, there's a strong smell of salt and seafood on this summer evening. It's drizzling now, a rain so soft you can't feel it falling yet, although you can hear it faintly in the bushes.

Highway 50. Main Street, truck route, lifeline. Centralmost of the cross-country U.S. routes but littlest known. The stories on

Highway 50 are varied and often quirky, the people protective: What they have is of great value simply because it has resisted change for so long.

Driving back, the only way the road goes, into a rush of headlights, I spot a person standing on the shoulder. A hitchhiker, traveling east. The highway rolls on.